GRIEF'S GARDEN

A True Story of Heartache and Estrangement

TABLE OF CONTENTS

DEDICATION

The time and effort in producing this manuscript and the life story that evolved is dedicated to the loving memory of Linda Marie: a beautiful person and spirit who was the original author of four most precious and special individuals.

ACKNOWLEDGMENTS

While the inspiration to write this book was living an impossibly unrehearsed life which included much that was splendid and much that has been challenging beyond my wildest imagination, it was the support from around me that made it a reality—beginning with my wife Jodi, who suffers my sufferings tied to her unending love. Her support, sense of logic, compassion and encouragement have been a never ending source of strength.

Copyeditor Ann Mauren has been a dream assistant: vigilant in keeping me on course and always ready with a suggestion or piece of advice. Thanks also go to graphics designer Amanda Matthews, who barely needed more than one take to arrive at the finished cover. And many thanks to Tricia O'Malley for her guidance through the maze of the self publishing scene.

I also acknowledge and thank my many friends for their respectful interest and understanding as they witnessed my efforts and trials over thirty-plus years while raising my family, and who were shocked and disappointed at the estrangement from my children, but ever loyal and supportive despite it all. I thank them for their unconditional caring.

INTRODUCTION

Help us be ever faithful gardeners of the spirit, who know that without darkness nothing comes to birth, and without light nothing flowers. —— May Sarton

Grief's Garden begins with a devastating revelation: my beloved wife and mother of our four young children has been diagnosed with ovarian cancer. When she loses her battle to live, a new battle begins as I struggle to move on with raising our family while trying to become whole again as an individual.

This story recounts my unique efforts to support and raise my children, my pursuit of family stability and emotional happiness, and the frustrating obstacles I encountered when attempting to blend families. With a timeline spanning twenty years, each episode provides an intimate, fascinating view of family dynamics and individual personalities that climaxes in heartbreak when I suddenly become estranged with some of my adult children.

An agonizing mystery and game of keep away ensues when three of my four children take shocking measures to shut me out of their lives. In my search for answers and a path to reconciliation, I explore the underlying issues of pathological grief, detachment, entitlement and arrested development. I also examine the roles that professional counseling and religious faith play in coping with the devastating effects of estrangement, a silent epidemic facing many families who are struggling privately with the pain, helplessness and embarrassment of a nearly taboo subject in today's society.

When my children were very young, I felt that cultivating a garden together was a great way to share lessons about growth and the cycle of life. It was a simple, easy to understand exercise to show how attention and effort could result in success. A garden offers magic right before your eyes in a time lapse sort of way. Successful gardening requires planning, soil preparation, seeding, planting, security like proper fencing to foil any furry purloiners, weeding, watering and fertilizing followed by more weeding and more watering and adding more soil nutrients. In retrospect, it became obvious that growing a garden is not much different than growing a family, which also requires planning, preparation, planting seeds, safety and security against the outside world, weeding out undesirable behavior, maintaining a steady flow of love, guidance and nutrition, all while keeping up a constant, attentive effort during your children's growth.

In our garden we grew sunflowers and some wild flowers along with zucchini, carrots, corn, peppers, melons, small yellow tomatoes and, of course, delicious red tomatoes: an absolute favorite right off the vine, especially after a run or workout. The kids were involved in the process. I wanted to share the magical journey a seed takes to its completion as a recognizable product that could be consumed for fresh nutrient benefits. Some plants don't make it or produce fruit. They are sometimes challenged by the conditions and are either stunted or die off. A garden is very much like life in that we absorb lessons about love, responsibility, compassion and hope along the way--sometimes when we aren't even aware that we are learning them.

Some of the names have been adjusted for privacy issues. I hope this true story of my growth helps others meet the challenges in their own gardens of life.

Thomas George

Erica cinerea

Bell Flower

Disappointment

1

THE DIAGNOSIS

1985 was to be a signature year in our life. Linda and I had four young children: Joseph, 3, Lynn, 5, Michael, 8 and Dan, 11. It was a major year for our family both personally and professionally. We already had our house for sale. It was a house we had just built six years earlier, and a place we really loved. It was literally across the street from the school and church in which we were members. That wasn't a coincidence. In 1979 there was one lot available in an older west suburban neighborhood that we were able to negotiate and build new construction because we wanted that convenience. To some, building a new house in an older neighborhood does not make the best economic sense because you essentially bring up the neighbors' value while compromising your own. But talk about great gas mileage! We had long memories from the seventies when there were gas shortages and rationing, and heading into the early eighties recession, we were careful with all our operating expenses. So living within walking distance to school, church and the grocery store a block away was as convenient as it gets.

But as our family grew to three boys and one girl it was decided that with only two bedrooms for the kids, and with three boys crowded in one of those bedrooms, we needed to consider moving to a larger house with four bedrooms. It's funny how we try to provide our children with more than what we had as children. I was from a family of ten and with three bedrooms: two for the children meant that there was a boys' room and a girls' room. With five boys it meant I had four roommates.

Those ten people also shared one bathroom that didn't have a shower or a sink. Still, I believe less was in fact more, as it taught us to share, be considerate, and manage our time and resources. Nevertheless, when Linda and I were raising three boys who had to share one room, we felt compelled to make what would have been a luxury for me growing up even better for our children. Since we were helpless as children, I believe it is the nature of parents to strive to improve conditions for our own offspring in an attempt to spare them from similar negative experiences of our own past. Unfortunately, we might also spare them from valuable perspectives and character growth that tend to accompany a life with fewer luxuries.

So early in 1985 we were fortunate to find that one buyer— as they say, one is all it takes—who paid us what we had invested in our property and allowed us to parlay that offer into new construction, which we began immediately. Our buyer needed to take occupancy in September, but our new place would not be ready for us until November, so we had to move into a hotel for six weeks. We selected a hotel in the vicinity of the new school that the kids would be attending. This would prove to be a character building exercise of its own as the six of us were compressed into a one room efficiency. With four young children quite literally under foot for what felt more like six months than six weeks, you can probably imagine the levels of relief and joy that surrounded our move to a spacious, four bedroom home.

Also, the fall of 1985 was when a major research project was ordered to determine a new format for the radio station I was managing. I had been in the communication business for seven years by this time and was managing a radio station that was struggling in its current format.   It was decided that an adjustment was needed to be more competitive and profitable. So with a business audible, selling our house, building a new house, living in a one room hotel, the kids starting a new school, and settling into a new community, there was a lot going on in 1985. With all of that Linda, and I decided to end the year by getting away on a weekend destination date.

Over the years, Linda and I were fortunate to receive workplace incentives when it came to travel. We had been to London, Acapulco, and Hawaii, but never to a much celebrated destination right here in the continental United States: Las Vegas. We had a friend that I knew from working with the same broadcast company a few years earlier who had been transferred to Las Vegas to manage an ABC affiliate television station, who was going to be our tour guide. So we made plans to check out the lights and visit the casinos in the desert. We were heading into our twentieth year together and because of all that we had accomplished during this year of transition we wanted to reward ourselves with a long weekend away in Las Vegas in mid-December.

After walking down that famous, glitzy, flashing strip, we were taken by all the lights and energy, but we quickly realized who paid the electricity bill: the gamblers. Neither of us had any experience with gambling. We weren't versed in Baccarat or even a game as simple as Black Jack, but we found our comfort zone in playing the one armed bandits: slot machines. The slots needed no tutorial; it was as easy as feeding the coins into the machine. We actually found one machine that was rewarding us for our time and money, paying out occasionally, at least enough to keep our attention. I'm sure after a couple hours we were no better than even. Then, with the dropping of three one dollar tokens, it hit the big one—at least for this machine. It paid out $400. For us, that was a big hit. I remember it ringing and dinging for the longest time directing everyone's attention toward us.

After our moment in the Las Vegas style spotlight, we gathered our winnings to take a break and sit poolside. Even as Vegas virgins, we knew that once you win you should walk away, otherwise you are just paying your share of that electric bill on the boulevard.

As it was winter, and the temperatures were in the low fifties, the pool area was vacant and quiet. It was a perfect, serene spot to escape the sensory overload of the casino buzzing on the other side of the glass doors. So we just sat there and basked in the low sun and the pure joy of knowing we rookie gamblers were up $400. We relaxed and talked: mostly about the kids, as parents tend to do when they are away. After awhile, though, I got antsy and rationalized that since we were way ahead, I'd just go back in and play our new favorite friend: the lucky slot machine. I told Linda, "I'm only taking $100 of the winnings to play with." After all, this machine was hot. I was gone for no more than ten minutes. When I returned, I wasn't embarrassed to say I lost the $100, knowing that we were still $300 up.

After sitting for a while, and getting antsy again, the same thing happened. I said "I'm just taking $100, and even if I lose, we'll still be $200 to the positive." This went on two more times until the $400 was back in the machine that first coughed it up. I guess it stopped being lucky. Even though we knew the ploy, we still fell for the gambler's trap: the allure that this was our lucky day after winning early. That was essentially the lesson of our trip and there was no need to have what we knew earlier to be reinforced: we did no further gambling—or utility bill paying.

What we did instead was track down our friend to guide us to the sites of Las Vegas. One particular point of interest for Linda was the hotel where Elvis Presley performed over 800 sold out shows: the Las Vegas Hilton. With 2,956 rooms and 305 suites, it was the largest hotel in the world when it opened in 1969. Our tour included a visit to room 3,000 on the 30th floor: the penthouse suite that Elvis called home when he was in town. Back then he would have the whole floor blocked for privacy and security reasons. I know it was a thrill for Linda to experience being in a place where "The King" performed and stayed. Elvis had died eight years earlier in August of 1977. We had been fortunate enough to get tickets to his sold out show at the Milwaukee Arena just a few months earlier in May of 1977—one of his last concerts. The performer we saw was the heavy Elvis. At the end of the concert he actually tripped down the stairs as the performance ended which gave a new meaning to the famous phrase "Elvis has left the building." But strolling the halls of the Hilton in Las Vegas—the same halls that Elvis walked—was a memorable experience, and one that I know tickled Linda.

Our friend also gave us an insider's tour of favorite spots that he and his wife enjoyed including the slot machine that was his wife's favorite. Out of respect we did not play that machine—out of respect for her and out of respect for our lesson already learned.

The next day was a Saturday and we just relaxed and enjoyed the quiet. It's funny to say that in a place like Vegas, but when you are raising four young children, quiet is a relative thing. That's something any parent will attest to. We were just enjoying our long weekend alone. We also enjoyed waking up late, a leisurely breakfast, and the entire spectacle that is Vegas. We shopped a little in the afternoon, had a late lunch and decided to catch a Saturday evening Mass, allowing us to sleep in on Sunday before our return to Milwaukee and the normalcy of life as busy parents. The church we selected to visit was about a mile down Las Vegas Boulevard. But it seemed a fast mile because of the many distractions that met us as we walked past all the lights and equally colorful tourists. At Mass I was surprised to see attendees put casino tokens in the collection basket. I realized then that tokens are the currency of Las Vegas—truly a world of its own. I pictured some altar boy from the parish being responsible for separating all the chips by casino and making the rounds once a week to convert the chips into cash to complete the contribution. While at church I was also reminded of a joke I'd once heard: what is the difference between praying in church and praying in a casino? In a casino you really mean it.

After our Vegas style Mass experience, which ended about 6 p.m., we took a nice, leisurely stroll back to our hotel as we had no agenda. It was during this walk that Linda was noticeably laboring. She was tired: tired on a day that had been as calm and leisurely as it could be—but she was struggling. I suggested that we flag a cab, but she insisted that she was fine to keep walking.

We were just a few blocks from our destination. Upon our arrival back at our room, she admitted to me that for the last few months she had felt bloated, and that she had distensions in her abdomen that concerned her. She also felt her weight was uncharacteristically high at about 130 pounds, when she was used to being in the 120 pound range. We talked about making an appointment with her gynecologist when we returned, but her response was that she mentioned these things to her doctor a few months back, and he was just going to say what he said then: that she'd had too many babies, this was the result, and just the way it was going to be.

Linda's doctor had the belief that one or two children were enough for a family. In fact, he and his wife only had one child. He was essentially transferring his beliefs and rules of life onto his patient. Instead of listening to Linda and performing a pap smear or an internal exam, he just sent her away with his own personal theory, without deferring to his professional knowledge. It took a fair amount of convincing on my part to get Linda to call and make that appointment. And when she finally called, the earliest they could see her was in two weeks on January 8th. None of us knew then the seriousness of the situation, so two weeks was acceptable. After all, she had just seen her doctor a few months earlier.

We got through the holidays—Christmas shopping, decorations inside and out, and Christmas concerts—without any idea of what was laying ahead of us. I always played Santa on Christmas eve, fabricating some reason for the kids that were still believers to excuse myself to a back room, put on the Santa outfit and sneak out the back. Then I would arrive at the front door with jingle bells to present a token gift with promises that if everyone went to bed early, Santa would return later that night with even more gifts. The holiday season progressed as usual, but it was special since this was the first one in our new house. The handmade, personalized stockings that Linda made for all six of us had a new home above a new fireplace.

Before we knew it, January 8th arrived, and we were on our way to the gynecology appointment. After his initial examination, the doctor knew immediately that something wasn't right. After the internal exam, he gave us instructions to meet him at the hospital the next day because he was admitting Linda for immediate surgery on what he determined was a tumor. The surgery was scheduled for mid morning at St. Francis Hospital, a facility we were quite familiar with since all four of our children were born there. We had lived just a few blocks from the hospital for four years in the mid 70s in our first home, and Linda had worked there as a candy striper while she was in high school. Linda's mom had worked there in the Radiology department for many years as well. And as a twelve year old, I had a tonsillectomy there. We were very familiar with admissions, checking out and walking the halls of the hospital. But on this day the place was destined to leave us with a memory like no other visit or stay.

I was in the waiting room down the hall. The surgery seemed to go on forever. I don't know if they started late, but it was an agonizingly long procedure and wait .After the surgery, the doctor poked his head into the waiting room, nearly empty except for me and one other gentleman. He asked if I would join him as we walked further down the hall where it ended at a bank of windows. I remember it was just after noon on a bright January day as the light crashed through the windows. He got to the point rather quickly explaining that they had performed a hysterectomy and removed a six pound tumor. I quickly processed in my mind the idea that a hysterectomy wouldn't have too negative of an effect since we had already determined that our family was set and we had no plans to have more children. In a flash I understood that Linda would probably have to take medications to compensate for surgically induced menopause symptoms that would soon follow—unpleasant, but manageable. But what I was unable to comprehend at the speed it was delivered was when he explained that the tumor was malignant. I wasn't well versed in medical terminology and I was trying to remember if malignant was the bad one, or if it was the other one that was the bad one. What was the other one called? Benign? But the doctor's demeanor gave me the answer: malignant is the bad one.

Linda was diagnosed with ovarian cancer, a silent, hard to detect form of cancer even to this day. She was to go home in a couple days, recover and heal from this surgery and then begin chemotherapy the next month. The doctor was intentionally vague about a prognosis, but I came to believe he knew more than he led on. But it was early; this was all new to us. Optimism is how I operate and I suspect I would have denied any negative prognosis anyway. But what I couldn't deny—and what I had to share with my children, Linda's mom and sister, my brothers and sisters, our friends and other family members—was that Linda had been diagnosed with ovarian cancer.

But that wasn't what was really really bad.

Quercus macrolepis

OAK LEAF

Strength

2

TEAM GEORGE VERSUS CANCER

Whenever it was one of the kid's birthdays we would do an age appropriate celebration of the occasion. Usually it meant a birthday cake made by mom and a gift along with a special dinner. If it was a special birthday, there would be friends or family included. But the best part was pulling out the close and play record player where we would play the Zoom Birthday song that was personalized for that individual. On January 14th it was Joseph's 4th birthday and Zoom, in that munchkin type voice—the one that sounds like he gulped helium—would proclaim "Joseph it's your birthday ... today!"

Linda had arrived home from her four day hospital stay still tender physically from her surgery and numb emotionally, still in shock from the news we received as a result of the surgery. Hearing the words *you have cancer* are only words. But when you string them together and try to process that this is your new reality, it just doesn't sink in and the emotional numbness persists.

The idea was to get home from the hospital and make Joseph's special day just that: special. We did not immediately reveal the cancer to the children. We were more vague about the finding. This was for a combination of reasons. We didn't want to spoil the birthday celebration; we didn't know how to share this with the kids; and I'm sure we were still a bit in denial thinking that the next day we would get a call saying there was a mistake. I'm not sure which reason was more dominant. Besides, we had at least a month before we had to explain why mom was going back to the hospital. The plan was for Linda to take five weeks to recover from her surgery so she was able to have the strength to begin the chemotherapy which would commence the third week of February. The chemotherapy treatment was based on some logarithm formula which would require ten months of treatment and hopefully that would have the desired effect of forcing the cancer to retreat. The last session was to be in November. The action plan was that Linda would be admitted the middle of each month for the chemo treatment and then take the end of the month to recover at home, which would supposedly leave her with the first two weeks of the month to be "normal" and not deal with the nausea. Within a very short time there was a new normal in our household.

There was a lot going on at this time. After all, we were just a few months into our new home and still getting settled. This had its benefits as Linda could distract herself with the details of setting up our new place. Getting her new kitchen organized, decorating and arranging each of the children's rooms, decking out the master bedroom and bathrooms and keeping up with the household activities. This was stuff that she was essentially able to manage during her two "good" weeks. The other two weeks of the month the household operation was my responsibility: laundry, breakfasts, lunches, clothes for school and covering all the kids' school requirements and extracurricular activities. I was fortunate to be in a management position as President/General Manager of a local radio station. This allowed me some executive privilege in being available to be present during Linda's treatments and to also be attentive to the needs of the children, taking over mom's duties two weeks of each month. And with the assistance of my dear mother-in-law—who was crushed by her daughter's diagnosis— we made it happen.

The hospital allowed me to remain with Linda during her chemo treatment. Then I would spend the evening and overnights with the kids. Sometimes we would all return to the hospital so the kids could visit with mom, and just their presence often was enough to give her the encouragement she needed to see each session through. During her recovery week at home, Linda's mother was available to assist her needs during the day while the kids were in school. I could catch up at work during the day and then spend the evenings at home doing laundry and keeping the house in order, and attend any scheduled after school activities.

Work had its own extreme challenges because on January 27th we announced a format change, which is a significant shift in operation. This change would require all hands on deck. As you change the format musically it also requires a complete re-orientation of the station involving talent and sales approach. It also affects all current advertisers as well as prospective advertisers. The marketing has to be re-executed to introduce the new product. It generally is one of the most time sensitive and frenetic periods in the radio business. We announced the change to our staff at halftime of a Super Bowl get together planned specifically for the purpose of making everyone aware of the format shift scheduled for midnight that evening. After much research we had elected a Classic Hits format featuring music of the sixties and seventies including artists like the Beatles, Rolling Stones, Billy Joel, Eric Clapton, Fleetwood Mac, and many others. The new venture at work made life even more demanding as we were attempting a new beginning.

They say when it rains it pours, and the storms in my business and personal life felt like a monsoon, showering me with more demands than I had ever known. It was a period of time when heavy expectations were made of me, not only emotionally, but also physically in servicing all the required needs of my family and employees. During the two "good" weeks each month, the sun would briefly peek out, and everything was as normal as we remembered. We could catch our breath and collect our sanity before the chemo treatment storms rolled back in.

During the first chemo treatment in February, they administered the cancer-fighting medication through a vein in Linda's arm. But quickly they determined that her veins would not hold up for the required ten months of therapy. Therefore, a week after her first treatment, she was readmitted so they could install a heart catheter into her left side, just above the ribs and below the arm pit. This would allow the chemo cocktail to enter directly into an area that would offer more immediate distribution into her system and prevent damage to her veins. To keep the line open and clean from build up, they gave us a tutorial on a procedure using a syringe to run saline solution through the catheter. Because the entry point was not convenient for her to do this procedure by herself, I would need to assist Linda with this on a daily basis This was just another stress point that she didn't need on top of everything else. It was another day where we all learned something new; we were growing just about every day in our new life.

As time progressed through the first months of treatment, we brought the kids into the discussion. With the older two (ages 11 and 8) we were a bit more detailed as far as what was happening. Reoccurring visits to the hospital were certain to pique their curiosity, so we explained the diagnosis and put a positive prognosis spin on it as best we could. We were more vague with the younger two (ages 5 and 4), explaining that mom wasn't feeling well and she was taking some medicine to help her feel better. We were finding that with a seven year range in ages, each child had a certain capacity to understand and process the information. We were just hoping that we were connecting. At this time Linda was also starting to lose her hair, and this would become conspicuous to the kids as well, so we needed to be as open as possible without unnecessarily scaring them.

Coming to terms with losing one's hair, especially for a woman, is traumatic in itself, though not as traumatic as the reason you are losing your hair. In the past, the idea of shopping for a wig had memories associated with something fun: variety and the possibility of expanding your look as an adolescent. So while there was a history in this area of wigs, it was not going to be a fun experience this time. Before, if you wanted a wig to experiment with, you got to keep your real hair. That wasn't the case here. Linda was losing hair with every brush stroke and in clumps as she would shower. This wig hunt had nothing positive attached to it, but it was a necessity. The bald look that an

23

occasional artistic woman might have the confidence to sport today was not in vogue in 1986. We settled on a short wig matching Linda's sandy blond color and left the store. It wasn't long before that wig became standard wear for her when she left the house, but at home she was content just wearing a scarf.

That summer we addressed the landscaping needs of the outside of our new home. As this was new construction, we had given the area some time to settle before doing any grading or planting. My father spent almost 40 years working evenings in a factory. His day job, when the season would permit, was grading, cutting out driveways, and general landscaping. He relied on both occupations during his life to support his family of ten.

In the summer of 1986 he was 63 years old and still active with his landscaping—which was more his passion—so he was able to assist with our outside makeovers. In a way it was a welcome distraction for our family watching Grandpa move the dirt around so we could finish our yard. When it came time to complete the landscape with rolls of sod, everyone got involved, including one of my brothers, a good friend, a neighbor, and my kids. Even as young as they were, they wanted to be helpful.

I can still remember my dad teasingly barking to the team rolling out the sod, "Remember guys: green side up!"

Laboring alongside family and friends almost made us forget what was really happening in our lives. We were all involved and working on the future by finishing the outside of our new home where we were all going to live for a very long time. It was a positive assumptive energy: we were contributing to our future as a family.

As August approached we had six months of chemo behind us. We were over half way there and by all measures it appeared to be accomplishing the goals. By that I mean the monthly rhythm had become familiar and Linda was able to get through it, so we felt we were doing our part allowing the treatment to do its part. Our focus shifted to the new school year that was to begin in a few weeks and all the preparation and planning that required. Again, another welcome distraction. It meant the kids were all going into the next grade, they were growing and our family was moving forward to better days. It also meant that the kids would be occupied at school during the week, reducing some of the stress of those two "bad" weeks each month. Even our youngest, Joseph, having turned 4, was going to spend a few days each week in preschool for the first time. We were heading for that time of the calendar that most parents anticipate in offering a bit of relief with built-in structure.

As November approached we had all the confidence in the world that the ten months of chemotherapy was going to do its job. Our confidence was based on the notion that we were going to win this battle. There was never a place in our dream for our marriage and our family where we didn't grow old together; that was all we ever imagined. Cancer might have crashed through our pre-conceived dream, but premature death wasn't going to happen. We were steadfast in that it happens to other families, but not in ours. So as the months were crossed off on our way to getting a good report after our last treatment in November, we were already planning a follow up surgical procedure for December. This was to confirm the cancer had retreated and that we were on our way back to normalcy. Linda was already imagining re-growing her hair by spring and retiring the wig to the mannequin head where it belonged. We were optimistic.

I had a business incentive trip to New York City scheduled for 75 of our best advertisers. It was tied to the start of the Christmas shopping season at the end of November. Linda had a relatively uneventful treatment earlier in the month and said she was feeling fine. I suspect she was just getting better at recovery after her tenth session. Feeling reasonably confident, I led my group to the the famous Manhattan shopping district for a long weekend that was titled "Shop Till You Drop." We had just arrived in the early afternoon when I called home to check in with my mother-in-law to make sure things were still going well. In that short period of travel time things went downhill for Linda. I immediately made arrangements to catch the next fight home arriving home later that evening. The next day we met with Linda's doctor. Instead of talking about a follow-up surgical discovery to confirm positive results from the ten month chemo investment, we were talking about beginning an even more aggressive chemo treatment as soon as she recovered from the recent session. December and January were targeted as the two months of aggressive treatment with the intention of blasting the cancer in a shock effort to jump start and get Linda ahead of her current state. At a follow-up conference the next week, I pressed the doctor for an honest prognosis. It was time for honesty. Our confidence was flickering for the first time. What the doctor told us next pulled the plug on that confidence. He said the cancer had spread and the chance of survival was about 3%. A measly 3%! But even while reality was knocking at the door, through our peephole of hope we concluded that since someone represents that 3% , why couldn't it be us? It was going to be us because this was not what we planned. This end was nowhere to be found in our dreams of a family and life together.

Despite the dark cloud now looming, we pulled off the Christmas holidays as best we could. After all, we still had a couple of believers and the last thing we wanted was any negative association with a child's best holiday of the year. In early January we tempered our unrealistic optimism with a bit of reality. Just in case we were not going to be in that 3% miracle margin, Linda and I talked about her making some audio tapes for each of the children. These would express her love for them and provide some direction after she was gone. She also left me a 20 minute love tape that I have in a safe place. I can only imagine how hard it was for her to record these messages: telling your children and husband goodbye. To this day, Linda's faith and courage is an inspiration to me. She was amazing in completing this loving, lasting gift. She wanted the kids to have it as a legacy. It was all she had to offer if she was going to be gone shortly.

The good news was that Linda was able to be a full time mom for her children, giving them undivided attention and not having to share her time or efforts with a job outside the home. They each received motherly nurturing to the max. The bad news was that since Linda was a fulltime mom and not divided in her time at home and at a job, her absence was going to be even more extreme and noticeable. We already had a taste of that throughout the year during the two weeks each month she was out of commission for treatment and recovery. Her void and absence was conspicuous.

Another treatment was ordered for the end of February. We did not know at this time it was to be her last. We checked in February 28th. They confronted the cancer with one more aggressive blast. Linda handled it well, just as she did with all her treatments: with inspiring courage and an amazing, positive attitude. She didn't care what she had to do. She wasn't afraid of dying. She was a person with a very strong Catholic faith. In fact, she was my example and with stronger beliefs then I had. She was only afraid and regretful that she was leaving her children and leaving me with everything left to do and accomplish for our four precious angels.

On March 4th I fed the kids breakfast, made their lunches for school and headed over to the hospital—a routine that was second nature by now. But today I was bringing Linda home and we would determine what our next course of action would be to beat the cancer. I arrived at the hospital in time for the doctor's meeting with Linda. It was a short meeting after which he asked to speak with me outside the room; I assumed to talk about our next treatment. I assumed wrong. He told me directly that there was nothing more he could do for Linda and that she had maybe 60 days to live. I did not hear, or maybe didn't want to hear him, so I asked him to repeat what he said because I could not comprehend his words. He confirmed what he said the first time. I still had doubts that he was right or certain.

That was until I walked out to the hallway just outside Linda's room. While I was talking to the doctor the nurses were helping Linda check out. They were helping her with all her personals she would bring with her including some things that were needed every time and basically kept at the nurses' station. But they were handing things to me or placing some on her lap as she was already in the wheelchair waiting for me to steer her out of the hospital and into our waiting car. But it was here that I heard loud and clear what the reality was. It wasn't anyone's words but it was the actions of the attending nurses—people that we had come to know by name over the last twelve months. Caregivers we'd gotten to know as people with spouses, with children of their own. And of course, they'd gotten to know Linda, which was easy with her beautiful, welcoming smile and her heart of kindness. What was loud and clear were their goodbyes, confirming that this time was final. These professionals had been here before and unfortunately had seen this scenario many times. They knew what death looked like. Their tears, their long hugs and their sweet goodbyes to Linda screamed that this was almost the end. For the first time I did not deny what was true, what was inevitable. In almost a flash what we tried so hard to suppress was now innocently exposed. We walked quietly towards the elevator. I remember standing behind Linda's wheelchair in the elevator with tears welling up in my eyes. I didn't want her to see me. We were alone in the elevator. And at that moment we felt alone in life.

But that wasn't what was really really bad.

Rosaceae rosa

BLACK ROSE

Mourning Death

3

THE LAST DAY

On the way home from the hospital, I knew that this was most likely the last time Linda would be out of the house. With the prognosis of maybe 60 days and the effort it took for her to get the strength to get out of the house, I figured it was best to do the one thing we talked about but never did because we believed it wasn't going to be necessary—at least not in the near future. That was to stop at the cemetery to select a final resting place. Over the past months, when we would allow our minds to go there, we had discussed cemeteries in the area. We were in our early and mid thirties and this was never imagined to be a topic of discussion that needed to be addressed so soon. We spoke just briefly about the convenient location of Highland Memorial as a place of final rest because of its proximity. We both figured it made sense so that down the road the kids and I would have a short distance for visits.

It was early afternoon, and as the cemetery was on our way home, we made a stop there. We drove through the grounds to an area where we knew a plot was available: right near a statue of the Good Shepherd. We had a brief conversation; it still was awkward to talk about a cemetery plot even knowing what we both knew, but it was something we took the opportunity to finalize. I wanted Linda to have a voice in her final resting spot. As hard as it was, it seemed like the right thing to do. There were going to be plenty of singular decisions in front of me from this point on with raising the children. I just wanted to get feedback from her on such a permanent decision. She gave her approval and thanked me for doing this. I suppose it gave her a visual and completion of what was just in front of us. But either way she showed great courage. Unlike me, she did not break down as would have been most likely for someone else. She appeared resigned to this being the end. We left the property almost as quickly as we arrived. No need to linger or talk options because it really didn't matter. I had gotten the approval I needed to know I was doing the right thing. That's the thing about decisions that were waiting to be made. There was no handbook or procedure for this . When facing death, what is proper and acceptable when involving your spouse and involving your children? You have to hope you are a person of good judgment and then trust that your thinking is pragmatic and timely.

That Sunday on March 8th it was an unseasonably warm day where the temperature hit 70 degrees. I remember my daughter was at a friend's house down the block and they were hanging out in an indoor spa. I had been running errands with the boys while Linda rested. It just seemed like such a perfect day after a several hard winter months—unexpected and welcomed. It was to be the proverbial calm before the storm. The storm was to strike few days later on Wednesday, March 11th. It was the day Linda passed away. It was a blessing that she did not have to endure the doctor's estimate of 60 days . She was ready. Her quality of life was not quality and life as we knew it was already over.

At about 5:30 that morning I had granulated some pain management pills and put it on a spoon with water to help her ingest it. She was not able to swallow very well by this time, and it was the only way to administer the medication. I lay back down next to her, waiting for my 6:15 a.m. wake up alarm so I could get the kids up, then make their breakfasts and lunches for school, before I would get myself ready for work. When I picked my head up to get up I looked over and could see that Linda was very still and appeared not to be breathing. Her last breath was taken somewhere in that period . It was hard to know exactly. The continuous hum of the oxygen from the tank that assisted Linda's breathing—that had become a part of the furniture in our bedroom—had the sound of life itself, so it covered any last breath that was taken. But I knew something wasn't right . It's hard to explain, but it was almost as if I felt the void. I went to feel a pulse and then for a heartbeat, but I felt nothing. I thought maybe because it was so weak and hard to discern that I just wasn't sensing it.

Linda's mother—who had taken up in a first floor den converted to a fifth bedroom—was spending the recovery week with us, as she did every recovery period. She must have sensed the void as well, because she entered our bedroom and asked what was happening. I said that I wasn't sure, but I thought Linda had passed. It took Linda's mom to confirm what I suspected because it was still unexpected even though it was expected. I remember not knowing exactly what to do. I was never here before.

Instinctively I thought of two things. The first was to contact our parish Pastor, Father Tom, to administer last rights known as Extreme Unction. Even though the priest had made a house visit just a couple days before and had administered last rights at that time because of Linda's dire health, I still wanted to make it official, in almost an obsessive way, that she was "covered." My second thought was what to do with the children who were getting ready for school. Each morning when mom was home they would file into her room to give her a kiss and hug goodbye for the day, just as they had done when she was healthy. I made a decision that the best for them was to have them say their goodbye to their mother as usual and if any questions were asked I would say that mom is still sleeping. Again, with the hum of the oxygen that by now everyone was familiar with as a standard sound coming out of our room, it all appeared normal. I felt with all the follow up ahead of me on this day of Linda's passing, most of which I could only imagine having never been in this position, I felt it was better the children were occupied with school and not in line of site of the priest coming for last rights and the funeral home coming to claim their mother. It was a visual they did not need to have in their heads.

As it was, Joseph, who did not have preschool on Wednesdays, was in the living room and witnessed some men bring a gurney with a black body bag down from the second floor. Although he was not aware of his mothers passing at the time, later he was able to deduct what he saw. This was something I found out in a subsequent year.

As soon as the kids were out the door for the bus a little after 7 a.m., I jumped in the car to get the news to our priest. The church and school were only a short mile up the road (an important factor in selecting our home's location). I couldn't call Father Tom because he conducted a 7 a.m. Mass each morning, which would have already started. Weekday Mass was always held in the chapel because of smaller attendance. I waited just outside the chapel not wishing to be a distraction. As I stood in the open doorway, all the attendees were facing forward and Father Tom was facing me. I tried to make eye contact with him. Having failed, I left a message with a school secretary to have him call me as soon as Mass was over.

Father Tom arrived shortly after 7:30 a.m. to bless Linda. He reminded me of something he had told me during his earlier administering of last rights: that the soul lingers for hours after the physical body stops functioning and that we had more then covered her last sacrament of Extreme Unction. And with that knowledge in mind, he assured me that the children's goodbyes that morning were effective in communicating their love and wishes to their mother. This was important for me to know because months later my mother-in-law innocently shared that morning's timetable with the kids. The older children were upset with me as they felt duped into saying goodbye to their mother when she had already expired. Even though I explained the lingering soul belief, I'm not sure they ever felt it was fair. But the reality is they were all sleeping when their mother slipped away and that their goodnight kisses the night before was the best anyone could do.

This was one of many things done in the process of losing a mother and spouse that you just do the best way you know how. Again, there is no handbook or course that walks you through what is proper, or what is right or wrong. Every situation is new territory and I believe I responded to our situation as best I could. These were some of the hardest decisions and things I have had to do in my life. My head and my soul still hurt as I relive them in remembering and writing about that time.

After organizing the priest and funeral home to cover their responsibilities, we called Linda's only sibling, her sister Mary Ann, and then we proceeded to notify my parents, my siblings and friends that had been standing by waiting. It was good the kids were occupied in school for the day as they did not need to witness the decision process, the calls, the figuring out what to do next, the tears, and the immediate sadness and heaviness of the next eight hours. They would have more than enough opportunities to witness the reality of their mother's passing once they arrived home from school and throughout all the activities over the next few days to realize the finality of what had happened. They didn't need to be in the thick of things this day. And maybe even more so I needed them and their needs to be put on hold while I figured out what to do next and what to do after that. I needed the time that a day at school could buy for me. I went from the shock that this was the day, to numbness of what had become official just hours before, to deep sadness that the love of my life was forever gone. In between figuring what to do I cried … and I cried.

As the afternoon approached, I needed to be able to focus on the four heartbeats that my union with Linda had created with God's blessing. My first concern was how to tell my children. I called the school principal at noon and asked her to collect the kids after school instead of putting them on the school bus. I didn't want them to come home and forever have the association of this horrible news with some room in our house or in general with the place they lived. I thought it would be best to tell them in the small chapel at their school. A place they would seldom visit since their Mass activity was always in the big church. The small chapel would be quiet, intimate and appropriate as the house of God. So Joseph and I left home together to meet his three siblings in the St. John Vianney chapel.

I needed the words that would speak to each of them in a way they would all understand and transcend the seven years that separated the oldest from the youngest, something that a 12 year old would comprehend as well as a 5 year old. For the purpose of conditioning them over the last month or so, both their mother and I let them know the medicine wasn't working the way we had hoped. In talking to them that afternoon I believe the older two had a sense why I intercepted them from the bus, but the younger two thought nothing of it. I said to them that the medicine did not work and was not going to work, and that mom went with Jesus today and now she was in heaven with all the angels, forever to be their guardian angel. There was quiet leading me to repeat myself and say the same message using different words. At this there was still a bit of uncertainty, lack of full understanding, probably more so from the 5 and 6 year old.

If I would have just been able to say "mom died today" it would have been painfully clear to all at any age, but I chose not to present it that way. The fact was I could not say those words even if I tried.

We spent a good half hour in the chapel. After telling them what happened I let them ask any questions they might have, of which there were just a couple. Then we just talked about life and how it was good that for the first time mom would no longer have to endure those awful treatments and the resulting nausea. How she no longer had to worry about the cancer and how peaceful she was and how much she loved them. That in heaven she had all her hair back. I also told them about the tapes mom left for them and that some time in the next week or so we would all listen to them individually and share them with each other. We talked about what was going to happen the rest of that week as part of the funeral. I explained what the more immediate thoughts and plans were after the funeral, and how in spite of this unimaginable horrible thing that just happened, we needed to remain positive as best we could, that we had each other and we had each other's love. That I was here to love ,protect and provide for them and that I wasn't going anywhere. And also now they each had a guardian angel that loved them more than anything in the whole world. We went out for dinner afterwards, to have a much needed meal, but more so because I was delaying the inevitable: the first time they would walk into the house knowing their mother was no longer alive. Sure they walked into the house many times while mom was gone to the hospital for her treatments, and maybe it felt no different than that, but within a short period of time the consistency of her absence would drive home the finality and reality. On March 11, 1987 I had to do the hardest thing I would have ever imagined in my life: tell my four young children that their mother had passed to heaven and was no longer with us on earth. I could only imagine their reality, their pain, their confusion. Nothing can hurt a parent more than feeling for your children and feeling the pain they feel.

But that wasn't what was really really bad.

Rosaceae rosa

DRIED WHITE ROSE

Sorrow

4

THE FUNERAL WEEK

When we arrived home after dinner that Wednesday night, I knew there was a lot to get in order quickly. Linda had just passed that morning and the funeral visitation was planned for Friday evening with the service and burial on Saturday morning. My mind was going into responsibility mode organizing all that had to be done for the funeral and the children. It just wasn't fair that I couldn't even process my personal loss of the love of my life. It did help somewhat that I had time to condition myself over the last 14 months, but even then I didn't take the time to fully prepare as I was too optimistic of the outcome. That night I assured the kids that they were done with school at least through the rest of that week and possibly into the next week. We needed to be together, and I wanted to keep them close so I could observe their behavior and response to what life had just handed them.

There was no grieving father's guide for what would be best in the short term and, more importantly, what would be best in the long term as the kids processed this loss in their lives. As hard as it is to imagine in today's world, in 1987 there was no internet or Google to search for advice and guidance. I had to plan a funeral for my wife and their mother, and that is what I kept in mind as we were going through the next few days.

I've often wondered how others accomplish these complex and emotional tasks in spite of what just happened in their lives. The answer is: you just do. There are no options. You just have to get through it.

I decided to involve the children in some of the decision making, as this was their mother, and their loss as much as it was mine. Keeping their ages in mind, I settled on a meaningful, personal task for the kids: assembling a collage of photos to honor their mother. Though it is common today, this was a relatively new concept at the time, and something I'm so glad we thought to do.

The older two boys, Dan and Michael, had more input than the younger two, Lynn and Joseph, because the pictures had more relevance to them. This activity took place over the next day and served as a purposeful distraction. While it would be hard to disassociate why we were doing this project, considering each picture of Linda—some by herself, some with me and many with the children—offered a brief mental journey to the happier time and place of the scene. Still, the sweetness of the memories the pictures evoked were undeniably mixed with the sadness of our new scene in reality: a portrait of a family with a gaping hole.

I thought the kids should see where the burial site was going to be for their mother, so on Thursday we all made the trip to the cemetery. I wanted them to take in the final resting spot that their mother and I had selected, in the hope that a little familiarity with the surroundings before the graveside service would reduce the distractions of an unfamiliar place, and maybe ease the overwhelmed feelings they were destined to have in this place. We also went into the cemetery grounds office and I let the kids offer their opinions regarding the kind of grave marker we needed to select and also the wording to engrave on the marker.

We did the same thing with the arrangements at the funeral home—although this time including only the two older boys—so we could make final decisions on the style of the casket and some program decisions. Their involvement was not forced and no one resisted, otherwise I certainly would not have made either boy do something they just could not handle. They were willing participants. Linda and I already had talked about which funeral home to use, so that is why I was able to make the call the day before when she had passed. But I thought that it might be helpful to not only allow the kids a voice in something so important, but I also felt it was an opportunity to help them come to terms with the finality of what happened. And to that end I believe it worked, because no one ever set a place for mom at the table from that day on, and while we had open talks about mom and our memories, none of the kids asked when mom was coming home. And just maybe their guardian angel had something to do with their adjustment as well.

On Thursday we also had to run to the local boy's and men's warehouse store to update the dress clothes that would be worn to the funeral. It was the kind of thing that Linda would have done. Lynn had a couple of new dresses that I had picked out for her from Macy's at Christmas time . One was gray velvet, the other was red velvet. Both featured pretty white lace collars, so I just needed to find a couple of sport coats for the older two boys, because the ones they had they had outgrown. It had been a while since there was a first communion or other special event where they need something more formal. I also needed to get a fresh suit for myself, something that was dark and appropriate that wouldn't require much tailoring as I needed it the next day. I remember seeing a family there from our parish and school that lived a few blocks away. We did not know them personally yet as we were still new to the area but I recognized them and they recognized us. I felt them stealing looks at us as the word had gotten out quickly about Linda's passing. We were "that young family" who lost their mother. I could feel the gaze and their awkwardness in not knowing what to say; so nothing was said. But throughout the time we were in the store I would glance and see the parents and children peeking at us. Not sure what they expected to see; maybe us sobbing uncontrollably. There were going to be many occasions for that, but they just would not witness it while we were shopping for clothes.

When we got home, Linda's mom had dinner waiting for us. Afterwards we talked with the kids about the funeral Mass and the music mom would have liked and whether or not the two older boys would want to be the altar servers for the Mass. At ages 12 and 9, they were regular servers throughout the year and quite familiar with the duties. It was just a question of whether they would have the courage and emotional control to serve for such a personal ceremony in their life. They felt they could do it. In fact, they wanted to honor her in serving the funeral Mass for their beloved mother. So we arranged for that as well. We also had to decide if we wanted concelebrating of the Mass. Our pastor,

Father Tom, was the main celebrant, but we also were able to have our friend, Father Richard, join the ceremony as a concelebrant. He was a guidance counselor and teacher I first met in high school and had baptized Dan and Michael after they were born—the two boys that would be serving this same Mass.

The outline that was presented to us included selecting scriptures and readers of the scriptures. We decided on the readings and the music based on what we knew Linda had always favored. The pall bearers were going to be my father, my brothers Joe, Mark and Roger, my brother-in-law Tim, husband of Linda's sister, Mary Ann, and our good friend John. During the time Linda was doing her treatment we had asked John to be the guardian for our children should Linda not survive and I was to perish in an accident so he was very special. We decided on our friend Dave to do the readings. Dave was a professional on air announcer and read live for a living, so even though he was a family friend and had an emotional attachment, his professionalism carried him. We also had to select music for the Mass. As we were faithful Catholics we never missed weekly Mass. And there were songs that I knew were Linda's favorites. Songs she would comment on as we left church. One of her favorites was "Here I Am Lord" with these lyrics: "I the Lord of sea and sky, I have heard my people cry, All who dwell in dark and sin my hand will save. I who made the stars of night, I will make their darkness bright. Who will bear my light to them? Whom shall I send? Here I am Lord Is it I Lord! I have heard you calling in the night. I will go Lord , if you lead me. I will hold your people in my heart."

If Linda had survived the sixty days, the doctor suggested we would have jointly arranged answers for the Mass outline including readers, music and celebrants. We would have found a way to select a casket, to select a grave marker and attend to other necessary details. It was a slower, more manual time with no world wide web and no convenient, online options back then. Despite that, in a way, going through the motions together and in person was actually better because back then we talked and we listened, so I knew full well Linda's tastes and she knew mine. And while we had some preliminary discussions about cemeteries, funeral homes and other details we never fully accepted what turned out inevitable until that last time in the hospital. And as we were home during the week she typically recovered from a treatment, we thought we would have more time to sort out all the details. Instead, we never got close to sixty days, so it was a blessing that we knew each other as well as we did, and I was able to fill in the outline of the funeral arrangements, with the help of our children and her mother who all loved her dearly.

Linda had a smile and personality that lit up a room. She was a person of kindness and compassion. A spectacular wife, a superb mother and a wonderful friend to many many people. On Friday evening the funeral home was bursting with attendees of the visitation. A line of family and friends stretched out the door and as far as the eye could see. All of them wanting to express their condolences and love. It still seemed unreal and unfair that this beautiful young mother of four was not going to be there anymore for her children, her husband, her relatives and her friends. There was much grief that filled the funeral home that evening. The parade of well wishers and people expressing their sympathy seemed to go on forever.

Before the prayer service was to begin I checked on the kids, especially Lynn and Joseph. A family member had run out to get them some fish sandwiches and drinks from a fast food outlet because it was after 6 p.m. and they had already had a long day. Dan and Michael stayed with me in the reception line for a while. Lynn stayed nearby when her aunts and uncles weren't looking after her. And Joseph did what 5 year olds do: run around and hang with cousins and friends that showed up. He was reasonably oblivious to the theme of the gathering. He was, after all, only 5. I also remember stepping outside for some fresh air to find out it was snowing—in March. And it was coming down pretty good. Just days earlier it was 70 degrees and sunny, but now it was snowing—that heavy wet snow that clings to the trees. I hoped it didn't cause an accident for people leaving who were emotional and teary eyed.

The prayer service lasted about 20 minutes. Everyone there had been encouraged to leave a personal note for the children talking about something they remembered about Linda or a memory they had that made them smile. It seemed as though everyone obliged because at the end of the night there was a box stuffed with notes from family and friends that the kids were able to take with them. We would eventually take time the following week to read through them all.

After the service was over and everyone filed out, they allowed just me and my children to sit and spend some quiet time with Linda. The kids joined me for a while and then it was just me. I remember seeing the love of my life in the pink dress she had selected to be buried with. I contemplated the personal effects we included in the casket and the wig on her head—the one she was planning to retire in the next month or two because her hair would have been back and thicker . In a flash, so many memories went through my mind: beginning at 14 years old and meeting her at that freshmen dance on a very snowy night in January all the way down to tonight, our last evening together on earth where it was snowing once again.

It was a very long day for everyone. Activity unlike anything we had experienced before. Talking to so many people had taken its toll. You end up feeling bad for them feeling bad for you, and awkward on their behalf when they don't know what to say, because there isn't much to be said. We all were very tired and I had no problem convincing the kids to get some sleep. Tomorrow, the day of the funeral service, was going to be another long and emotional day. I had just lain down and was in the early stages of sleep when my daughter came into my room and said she wasn't feeling well and felt like throwing up. We weren't able to make it to the bathroom before she started to vomit. I first thought all the emotions of the day wore her down and made her nauseous. But I also considered that the food she ate might have made her sick or it might have been the flu—the 24 hour variety. Whatever the case, it was an instant confirmation that this was my new life. No luxury of saying "honey, I'll clean up the floor if you clean up the kid." It was me and only me. I cleaned up the mess made on the way to the bathroom. I cleaned up Lynn and soothed her with some children's Pepto

Bismol, then helped her make her way back to bed—all the time wondering if she was going to be well enough to make it to her mother's funeral in the morning, and if not, how would I handle that as all friends and family would be there with no one to stay with her. But like most things in life, I worried for nothing, as thankfully she was fine in the morning.

I made breakfast in the morning wanting them all to have something substantial in their stomachs as it was going to be a long day. Then I made sure everyone was dressed as planned. Months ago, while she had the ability, Linda showed me how to use the curling iron on Lynn's hair. I had done it a number of times since then and actually thought I did fairly well having received Linda's and Lynn's approval. Each time when I was done, Lynn would look in the mirror with me over her shoulder and I would proclaim "A masterpiece!" Today was a day that I needed to produce another masterpiece. Thankfully, the three boys had no hair issues other than an occasional case of bed head, easily remedied with some water and a comb.

We needed to be at the funeral home by 9 a.m. to allow for a last private visit before they would seal the casket. There was to be a brief prayer service at 9:30 a.m. before the procession to the church and the funeral Mass. At the funeral home service, an old high school friend of my dad, Father Gene, a Jesuit who was a bit of a celebrity with his own long time weekend TV show called "All You Need Is Love" did a brief prayer. I remember him saying Linda will always remain alive in our hearts and that now we have a new saint to pray to: Saint Linda.

The four mile funeral procession to the church was memorable. Time almost stood still as the kids and I were all in the car immediately behind the hearse. The wet snow from the night before clung heavy to the trees and the last mile before the church was lined with old oak trees that had grown over the road. The beautiful white snow clinging to the branches created an amazing sparkling canopy as we drove underneath, symbolizing a cover of protection—at least it felt that way now with Linda looking down from above.

When we arrived at the church the older two boys immediately went to the sacristy to get their altar boy cassocks on as Lynn, Joseph and I followed the casket into church. The service was emotional as expected. I remember crying though most of it realizing that this service was really drawing us near the end. My daughter looked up at me and I tried to be strong, but I was not successful. Later she remarked that she never saw me cry before, which was a statement in itself. At the end of the Mass I wanted to honor Linda with a eulogy of my own. Quickly I relived the highlights of our twenty-plus year relationship, focusing on her gifts to me: our children. In life I would always say to her that no matter what I provided for her or accomplished in life, I could never match or pay her back for what she did for me, which was to bear, nurture and give the foundation to our children, which she did so lovingly. And now with her passing I could at least come close in measuring up by accomplishing the dreams and goals we shared in raising our children with the quality education, the health, safety, nutrition and opportunity that she aspired for all four of her children. My indebtedness was to fulfill her will.

We proceeded to the cemetery, which looked somewhat different than it had a couple days earlier with a blanket of snow. There was a brief prayer service with a blessing, everyone sprinkling holy water in the form of the sign of the cross, and everyone taking a flower from the splash that rested on the casket. Then we returned to the church where the women of St. John Vianney provided a luncheon reception in the lower level of the facility. It was so very kind, and many of those women that hosted us, along with their husbands, became some of my best friends, whose companionship I still enjoy today.

After talking to many people, allowing them to express their condolences and bewilderment, I gathered the kids and went home. We settled in for a bit, but a couple of hours later, before it got dark, we went outside for a walk up the block to get some fresh air and to do something together as a family—a newly redefined family of five.

The date was March 14th. And as we walked along the slushy roadway, the subject came up of what we were going to do for my birthday which was the next day. We decided that we weren't in a celebration mood and it should be low key. One of the kids asked how old I was going to be. I responded that I would be 35 years old. At that, Lynn expressed concern because her mother, who was nine months older than me, had died at age 35.

She exclaimed, "Oh no, Dad! That means you are going to die now!"

My reassuring response was, "No Lynn. Look at Grandma and Grandpa and how old they are."

I explained that it was very unusual for someone to pass away at her mother's age. But it taught me quickly about the fear they had of losing their other parent and of being orphaned. In a way it would be like living with one kidney and under constant, traumatic threat of losing the other.

A few years later, my oldest son wrote a poem for a class project titled "Death."

It never hits home
Only down the street
To the neighbor or a friend
But never to you

But the truth is that it does
In the worst of times
In the biggest surprise
But never to you

The earth turns black
Life is grey
Nothing to live for
On that particular day
But never to you

But then you realize

It does happen to you

Now you know when your father cries

Especially when your mother dies

Emotions fly in a furry

And life seems so dreary

But then you realize

You must go on

Why? Because ...

I love you Mom.

The funeral week in saying goodbye to the love of my life, and keeping a watchful eye on how each of the children were handling and processing this horrific loss, and everything that death, funerals and moving on represents was by far the hardest week of my life to date.

But that wasn't what was really really bad.

Syringa vulgaris

WHITE LILAC

Youthful Innocence

5

VIRTUALLY MARRIED AT 14

In the fall of 1966, I had enrolled at Pio Nono High School. It was Latin for Pius IX, and since there was already a Pius XI High School in the area, to avoid any confusion they maintained the Latin version. How my father managed to afford his goal of sending all eight of his kids to parochial elementary and high school—and the tuition that required—on a meager factory salary is beyond me, but it taught me early that if you want anything, you have to support your beliefs by being committed to your goals and work hard. As a high school freshman I was just trying to find my place among a new student body. None of the kids that I went to grade school with joined me at this high school. I liked sports, so I knew I wanted to get involved there, and student government interested me, and, of course, girls! But going to an all-boys school, it was not going to come easy, or so I thought.

There was an all-girls school, St. Mary's Academy, just a half mile away. The only thing that separated the boys and girls was a major seminary for men preparing to be priests. The half mile (and the courage to talk to one of the girls) was all that separated us. It was January 26th, 1967 and the all-girls school was sponsoring a freshmen/sophomore dance, allowing an opportunity for the opposite sex to meet one another in a controlled environment. My older sister Sue, who was a big Elvis fan, was kind enough to take me into our living room, when no one was looking, to teach me to fast dance—or at least fake it. I figured I could also shuffle my feet enough to pull off a slow dance if needed. Truth was, I didn't plan on using either skill; I was hoping I could just blend in and observe this first mixer to see what it was all about. But about midway through the evening a sophomore fellow student of mine that I had gotten to know a bit was introducing me to this girl he was seeing, and also to her friend. Her friend was a sophomore as well and introduced herself as Linda. She had this aura of maturity about her that gave her an appearance of being much older. She was beautiful; she was stunning. And I ... I was a freshman still looking for my confidence. But somehow amidst all the loud music from the live band playing we pulled off a brief conversation. Maybe it was one of those times when you really only pick up every other word but you politely smile with an occasional nod of the head. Whatever it was, I sensed I didn't make a bad impression and that included only being a freshman. We went our separate way for the next set of music but we bumped into each other again later in the evening as she was just standing with her friend taking in the music. I said hi again, and we chatted briefly while they started to play a song on which I felt I could try my newly learned dance moves. It really wasn't much of anything but a sway from one side to the other while swishing my hands and arms out to the side, which in itself didn't require the confidence, but it was asking this gorgeous woman—a sophomore—to dance. I summoned the courage and she said, "Sure!"

After the dance, as luck would have it, they played a slow song and since we were still engaged in conversation, I was on a roll and asked her to dance again. And once again, she said, "Yes."

I was careful not to step on any toes. After the dance we talked some more, just small talk as the evening was coming to an end. I had her first name so I asked for her phone number, and if I could call her sometime. She declined to give it to me, as she would eventually tell me, not because she didn't want me to have it, but because she was raised to be a proper girl which meant not giving out her phone number. I asked for her last name, figuring I could look it up. She gave it to me. In fact she had to spell it out because there was a silent e in the middle of it. She left the building to catch a ride from her father and I headed for the bus stop. I remember standing at one of my connection points on a two transfer ride .It was snowing: a gentle fluffy snow. But all I could think about was this incredible person I'd just met. I was flying high. Besides the snow, destiny was also in the air.

I know it sounds ridiculous, but I was 14 and I felt I had found the love of my life, even though I had no idea if she would have any interest in me. You know how some people fall head over heels and say they can't get that person's face out of their mind? Well mine was different. I was so taken by her beauty, gentleness, kindness and easy personality that I could not picture her face . This feeling was just so huge that I couldn't comprehend it. When I arrived home, I quickly went to my sister's yearbook, as she was a senior at the same school, to look up Linda. And there she was!

Some people know early on in life what they want to be. That wasn't me. I also did not hang out with the guys at pool halls or drive around with a few buddies in the car flirting or looking for some action. What came from within me was that I wanted to have a relationship. Not date different girls, just one special girl. If she was very special, all the better. Linda was that person. Certainly it wasn't on my checklist at 14, but there she was. I don't fully understand why I was built that way to seek out a life companion so early, but that was who I was and who I continued to be even after Linda's death. I liked sharing my life with someone special. I liked the companionship and the balance it contributed to the rest of my life. I liked being married as I was virtually married at 14 years of age.

We dated, mostly using the public bus line at that time, and occasionally doubling with someone who had a car. We would go to movies. Our first movie was Fahrenheit 451 at the Downtown Grand Theatre. We went bowling and took walks along the bluffs of Lake Michigan which was right across the street from her high school. In the winter we would go ice skating at an outdoor flooded and frozen lagoon and then go for a burger and shake at a favorite diner. I didn't have much money as I was only able to work on a produce farm until I turned 15, and then worked as a short order cook and dishwasher at a drive in restaurant. But we didn't require much entertainment. We did what we could afford to do and we were content. We attended school plays and sporting events. We went to more school dances. We were the King and Queen of our high school prom, and Linda was the Homecoming Queen as well. High School years became quickly defined for me: Linda and sports were my focus. In classes that were boring I would either day dream about Linda or sometimes mentally calculate my quarter mile splits for the two mile race. By my junior year I was Conference and State Champion in the 2 mile. Getting acceptable grades was the obvious purpose of going through high school, but Linda and sports were my positive distractions and what gave me balance. I learned early on how important balance was in being able to perform in all facets of one's life. The sports involvement, specifically the distance running, conditioned me for trials that awaited me later in life. The endurance lessons I experienced while crashing through barriers in training and distance racing would serve me well as there would be many unknown obstacles ahead which I was going to have to transcend and conquer by enduring what life would throw at me.

Linda and I were from the same side of town. We shared the same values, and the same strong Catholic faith, although in truth she had the stronger faith of the two of us, and was my moral compass. She was the better person. We both also had parents of strong faith as positive role models. That was especially the case with her mother and my father. We came from modest lower middle class back grounds. We were both respectful and had an appreciation of all that we received. We were careful with money as we managed our minimal funds, rather than let it manage us. We were good at saving up for what we needed and sometimes even what we wanted. We were both low maintenance. I was more sports minded and Linda more musical with a superb voice that only lacked the confidence to share its beauty.

She was well-liked by my mother and father. The only thing that ever served as a speed bump was my father's suggestion that I should perhaps date some other people for the simple purpose of comparison. Since Linda and I were exclusive starting at age 14, I never had (or wanted) the opportunity to date anyone else. This wasn't a rejection of Linda on his part, just a father being practical since he could see us heading toward an engagement. Even though I was the third oldest of eight children, I was the first to break the seal and date steadily.

Linda was especially wonderful with kids, more specifically with my younger siblings, four of which were between 3 and 8 at the time I met her. I remember there were times she would come over to our house and they would get her on the floor to color with them; they really liked her and she them. In fact, I have to admit there were times I was a little jealous and would declare that she came over to visit with me and to stop bothering her. Of course, it was no bother for her, it was just me feeling neglected and having to share my girlfriend.

We got engaged the summer after I was out of high school. Not that I was going that far away to college , only 40 minutes south of where we lived, but it just seemed inevitable. We did not set a date of marriage as Linda went into the work force for a well-respected bank in the area right out of high school, and I wanted to get some college and direction under my belt before planning a date. But after a couple years of college, we were just running back and forth every weekend anyway so we figured Linda could secure employment at a bank in the area where I was going to school and we could make our life simpler by being together. Just living together was not an option, and would disappoint our parents, which we would not want to do , so we set a date and married in the middle of my junior year in college during Christmas break on December 16, 1972. I was 20 and Linda was 21 years old. It was a bitter cold day with wind chills near zero degrees, but the air was crisp and the sun shone brightly.

About two months after our wedding, Linda found out she was pregnant. This was news that we were unprepared for. We had just married, Linda had just moved to a new area, in a different living space, taken a new job and now she was pregnant. It was a lot happening all at once in her young life. I remember coming home from school that day and Linda was preparing dinner in the kitchen of our small efficiency unit. She was crying because this was not the plan. We were going to start our family after I graduated and had a job. She was in the middle of so many transitions and now she was going to be a mom. She ended up having a miscarriage about ten days later and then felt guilty as though she had somehow willed the miscarriage. With her misgivings and upset, she believed that the fetus had felt unwelcome, and thus the miscarriage. Of course that wasn't true—unless you believe it, and that is what Linda believed.

As she recovered, she learned from hospital personnel how common miscarriages actually are—something neither of us knew—and that it was the body's way of short circuiting what it determined would be an unsuccessful pregnancy. These assurances made Linda (and me) feel a little bit better. But this event was to change our complete timeline. Because of the residual guilt Linda still felt, she now wanted to have a good pregnancy sooner than later, something we worked on once she received her doctor's clearance.

Not long after, she did get pregnant and delivered our first born son, Dan, at the end of the summer of my senior year. I was a 22 year old dad, and had just graduated that May. However, with a recession dominating commerce, I had not started my career as I was unable to secure a job. But our family was started, and if you are planning to have multiple children, generally you want to space them relatively close to one another for their mutual companionship, but also to assist the flow and pace of raising them as you are in the rhythm of parenting.

Linda and I thought we were in control and making calculated decisions on when we would start our family and continue its expansion, but all the while our Creator knew Linda's time on earth was short, and that she would be gone by 35. Still, he allowed her the youth and time to deliver four healthy children, giving them the gift of life, and the gift of their mother's nurturing care during the first five formative years of their lives. We were all truly blessed, and Linda and I were blessed to have enjoyed twenty years together. It was a supreme gift from our Supreme Being.

Linda had one sister and I had seven siblings, which is probably how we arrived at having four children of our own. We actually thought five was the right number early on, but during the pregnancy with Lynn, our third child, Linda experienced placenta previa, which is where the placenta attaches itself to the cervix and as dilation slowly begins, the placenta is at risk of rupturing, causing a premature birth and serious bleeding. So Linda was bed-ridden the last two months of the pregnancy. This caused a number of hardships, but it was important to keep Linda off her feet to get her to full term. The doctor advised against having any more children because of the risk of another placenta previa situation. But Linda became pregnant with Joseph not long after, and to our dismay, it was a partial placenta previa.

After Joseph's birth we took precaution from further pregnancies as we felt we were pushing our luck, and settled at an even number of four, feeling every bit blessed that our creator graced us with four healthy children.

During the raising of our children while Linda was alive there were challenges not unlike most families. But as their parents, we shared the same goal of raising healthy well-adjusted and respectful human beings. There were complications and emergency room runs with all the kids. Our youngest, Joseph, had to wear casts on both of his legs to stretch his heel cords because he wasn't walking at the normal time for development of that skill. This was followed by wearing leg braces while he slept for a period of time afterwards.

Our oldest, Dan, had to have his ear surgically addressed because the cartilage did not develop as expected. Runs to the emergency room included the time Lynn jumped off a bunk bed and bashed her mouth into a dresser. With all the blood it appeared that she had knocked out all her teeth. Linda and I were freaked out, but it all healed and was to be okay.

Our second son, Michael, was two, he tripped over a raised sidewalk, hit his head and developed a goose egg sized knot that required an emergency run. There were other emergency runs throughout the years in response to running into a fence sled riding, or hitting a head on a fireplace hearth requiring stitches, but all in a day's work as a parent; part of the territory and torture of trying to raise your offspring safely.

Besides the diapers, the daytime and late night illnesses, and the constant vigil to maintain safety, there were so many wonderful family experiences. Annual family days at Great America theme park, at Noah's Ark water park, at ball games, sled riding and skating during the winter, days at the beach at local water holes and public pools, cub scouts, brownies, little league baseball for the older two boys, school plays and programs, family pictures scheduled, birthdays and so many day in and day out experiences just in the back yard that Linda and the kids were able to share before she passed. Not nearly enough (it probably never is), but in appreciating what you have and not dwelling on what you don't have, we were blessed many times over with quality family time along with so many pictures and documentation that has been recorded and left behind to remind us of the gift of family and happier days with Mom and Dad

Artemisia absinthium

WORMWOOD

Bitter Absence

6

FIRST FEW MONTHS AFTER THE FUNERAL

After the kids were in bed the night of the funeral service, I lay awake in my bed for a few hours. My mind grappled with all that had transpired the past week and especially with the fear of the unknown of what laid ahead of our family. It was daunting, but I was determined to not be overwhelmed. I remembered what Mother Theresa said. She spoke the often quoted words "God never gives you more than you can handle," but she followed it with, "I just wish he didn't have so much confidence in me." It made me chuckle quietly in a nervous way. Even in your most troubled time, you need to find it within yourself to keep things in perspective—as hard as it may be—and keep the bigger picture in view. There was one other time later that year when I looked up to the heavens and softly chuckled at myself. It was when I received some good news at work. As I had done so many times before, I swung around to my credenza where my phone was to call Linda to share the news. I actually had the phone in my hand and was ready to dial when reality caught up to me. I smiled, looked heavenward and said in a soft voice, "Oh, that's right. You already know."

The day after Linda's funeral was Sunday, and it was my 35th birthday. We went to church as a family, as we always did, but this would be the first time without Mom in the pew with us. As the service progressed, I felt many eyes landing on us. We were that family. On top of all the sorrow and mourning, I felt uncomfortable for others who didn't know where to look or especially what to say. The fact is there is nothing worthwhile to say. There is nothing that they can do to change what happened. However, a number of fellow parishioners made meals and dropped them off, which was greatly appreciated. But no one can abate the sadness, the emptiness, or the loneliness brought upon a family by such a significant loss.

Of course, prayers were always welcome, and these became the filler while days passed. Time elapsing was what it would take to soften the blow; realizing the loss never gets covered or filled. Unfortunately, there's no time machine that speeds you past the empty, painful days and deposits you in a happier place. No, you just have to weather that dark heavy cloud that hovers and sometimes even presses on your shoulders. I suspect some of that feeling was the shock of what actually happened. But over the years, little by little the cloud does begin to dissipate, even if it never disappears entirely.

We came home and had a very subdued birthday acknowledgement, since, after all, no one was in a celebratory mood. But I still felt it was important as a signal that life would go on, and that we would do the kind of things we did while Mom was alive. That notion became my goal: beginning with day one, life would go on and we would do what was done before and keep the traditions initiated by their mother and me, and move ahead as normally as possible.

The following week the kids took some time off from school, as I did from work. It wasn't going to be easy for them to return to school or for me to go back to work, but the first day back was inevitable, so without a drastic delay we all returned to our schedules the subsequent week. My oldest son had a basketball game scheduled the following weekend. I asked him if he felt up to playing. I left it up to him guessing he would want to play and knowing that as soon as we got back into our former routine the better it would be for all of us. So we all attended the game as a family to watch him play and set a subtle example for the rest of his siblings.

To assist our moving forward, I sought out a 6 week program conducted locally by St. Joseph's Hospital. In those days, resources for the grieving were sparse. This was a pilot program for those that had suffered a recent loss. It was not specific for any particular loss. If you lost a grandparent you were welcome; if you lost a pet you were welcome; if you lost a parent you were welcome. So while it was not specifically targeted to grieving spouses or children, it was a nice way to address what we had just experienced and as we were in our first couple of months without Mom, I wanted to get some kind of professional assistance.

The program at St. Joseph's was helpful. There were a number of exercises that were presented. One in particular required that each attendant to draw a picture of their family. It provided a snapshot of how they perceived things now. It helped to determine if anyone was in denial. My daughter drew a picture that included her father and three brothers. She even included her brother's hamster. She had a sun in the sky and next to that she had drawn a heart. When asked by the moderator what the heart represented, she explained that the heart represented her mother because her mother would always be in her heart. While it was an early sign, I took it as a healthy sign of what was to be a long process of adjusting.

Another sign I considered as healthy was a piece my youngest son (who was about seven at the time) wrote in school a few years later. The title was "Once Jesus Came to My House," and it read like this:

Once Jesus came to my house. I asked Jesus if I could see my mom and he let me see her. So me and my mom hugged each other. Then we made dinner: potatoes and pork and lemonade to drink. We had lots of fun. Then I asked him if I could see my grandpa. Jesus said yes. Then he joined us too. It was fun. Then I asked him if I could go up to heaven. Jesus said yes. Then Jesus gave me a red thing and Jesus said it that it would make me strong and powerful and it will make me live forever and ever and I will always win games. After that we had desert. Then Jesus said well, since we are up here, why don't we have a party? Me and my mom danced a little bit. Then we ate some cake and we went to bed.

For the last year or so, while Linda was receiving the monthly treatments and then building her strength back through the recovery period, I stepped in to do some of the laundry, grocery shopping, breakfasts, school lunches, school responsibilities and various family errands. So to care for those things full time and keep up with my employment responsibilities certainly put pressure on me. But the previous 14 months helped to condition me for the process. Linda's mom was available to help out some of the time, but she was a widow in her late sixties with a pacemaker and limited energy. And she was grieving too; she had been very close to her daughter. I didn't want the stress of running a household comprised of four young children to further damage her health.

The older children continued to be of help with folding the laundry, loading and unloading the dishwasher, taking out the garbage, and other household chores. To help me see the positives, I remember thinking what other fathers would know their children's size of underwear, shirts and jeans? And what other fathers know all the teachers and other moms from school meetings and activities? Probably not many, maybe none. Those thoughts helped me to consider my situation as an opportunity that I wouldn't otherwise have had, and that I was lucky to be in a position where I knew so much about my own children.

A few weeks after the funeral we all pulled out the tapes that Linda had made for each of us. They were produced by Linda as something we could always refer to and listen to her voice for guidance as we moved through life. It was an eerie feeling to hear Mom's voice for the first time in weeks, knowing she was no longer with us. But in a way, it was exactly what Linda had in mind, and that was to let them know she was still present with her love, looking over everyone.

Each of the kids had the option to listen to their tape privately or to share it with the family. The message in each one was in the spirit of guidance to remind them that she loved them very much and was so sorry the medicine did not work. She wanted them to always love each other and to be kind to each other. No fighting. That they needed to help their father out now and listen to him as he was going to have his hands full. And that they needed to work hard in school, always doing their best. She encouraged them to love one another; that was as close as they could get to continue loving her while she was no longer physically around. She said that each one of them was a gift from God; that they were composed of half of their mother and half of their father, and to love and be kind to one another was to love and be kind to her. That last part of the message is what they seemed to have forgotten over time.

I also chose to share the beautiful tape Linda left for me. It was a 20 minute love note that spoke of her love for me, the difficulties that were in front of me as a single father of four, how she was so sorry to leave me alone. She said making the kids tape was hard, but her tape to me was nearly impossible in having to say goodbye. She wished she could send me a note from the afterlife letting me know why all this had happened to us. But her faith, which carried her, continued to come out in her message to me. She was appreciative to have the opportunity to be able to leave the kids and me our tapes. She thanked God for our life together remembering the good times as we grew up together during those early formative teen years. Accepting her plight was what God wanted and she figured she had enough good times. Saying I was just right for her and that she couldn't have picked a better boyfriend and then husband. How happy I made her in life. Her voice smiled for a moment when she said "I guess what I'm saying is thank you for asking me to dance." She repeatedly talked about how we were the best together and how she hated to go and that we should have had so many more years together to see our kids in high school, rocking grandchildren, family Thanksgivings and Christmases. She spoke of us being together when the kids were gone later in life. That it was a rotten shame we were being robbed of our life together. She spent much time apologizing for being gone and leaving me with so much. (Imagine that: to be sorry for something she had no control over.) That she was going to pray for me from above that I could handle everything that was waiting for me, and that if there were times I felt overwhelmed, to think of her and our dreams for our children to see me through. As I told her when things were looking bleak that there was a place waiting for her in heaven, she insisted in her tape that anybody having to be both a father and mother for four children deserved to be rewarded with heaven as well. She really wanted to be reunited in the afterlife saying that it is said you don't really recognize what we knew as earthly figures, but hoped we would.

She spent most of her message talking of our love and her love for me, saying she never felt so loved in her life and that I was her gift from God, and that I always made her happy. She called me a most wonderful husband and thanked me for a really, really beautiful life. She said that she was going to miss me, but she was going to be in a good place as she said it's those left behind that have the struggle. She also wanted to be sure to give me permission to move on in life. She unselfishly wanted me to be happy in life. She understood that I would be alone and she didn't want me to be lonely. And then, once again with a smile in her voice, she said that she would be looking down and be jealous, but if I found someone that loved me and our children, she would be okay as long as that someone could tolerate some pictures of her in the house, ending that comment with a little laugh. She closed by saying she hoped I would never have to use this tape, and that God changes his mind sometimes, and that she couldn't say goodbye to me, instead she said I love you forever; my love for you will never die; I will always love you. Love, Linda.

There were many times over the years I would listen to my tape for her love, appreciation and inspiration. Her forever love was critical in helping me get through many challenging times when I felt I was in it alone.

That spring we fulfilled a promise Mom had made to all the children during her last months of life: that Dad would take them all to Disney World. Because of the magic that Walt Disney created and a brand that is synonymous with fun, Disney World is a sure fantasy destination for any child. There were no illusions on anyone's part that a Disney trip made up for their monumental loss, but it was something for them to look forward to, something positive. It could distract from their sorrow for a short period of time, thus helping time pass and separate from their loss.

Through the kindness of our friend, Bill, owner of Mark Travel, who arranged complimentary roundtrip air travel to and from Orlando, Florida, we were able to spend ten days in the sunshine state that spring. We had a wonderful time, all things considered. We stayed in the Orlando /Disney area for seven of the days visiting the Magic Kingdom, taking in all the rides and attractions, and enjoying all that Disney had to offer. The five of us were able to escape, if only for that moment, from all that dwelled in our minds. We had great family time. We got a convertible and enjoyed rides up and down International Drive as we chanted in unison, "We are the Georges!'' We can't be beat! Clap your hands, stomp your feet!"

One particular hotel we would pass on our way to the Disney property was called the Peabody Hotel. For some reason the name struck them as funny and as we would pass it the kids would shout out, "The Pea...Body!" While in Orlando, the awakening of my new life made its presence felt again. Not only that there were four of them and one of me, and this was a first family trip with no Mom, but during our stay there was some swimmer's ear irritation that was causing a couple of the children pain and discomfort. I found myself heading to the drugstore late at night seeking a remedy and thinking this is all mine with no partner to share the good and the bad, the health and the sickness.

After seven days enjoying all that Disney and our hotel pool had to offer, we headed to the west coast of Florida to the Tampa Bay area where a couple of my brothers and their families lived. We had seen them at the funeral, but my brother Joe (who is seven years my junior) and I have always been somewhat close. It was nice to spend a day or so with family since we were in the state.

On Saturday morning we returned to Orlando to catch our noon flight back home. We wanted to get home on Saturday and have Sunday to decompress and get ready for school and work on Monday. We returned our rental car and took the shuttle to the airport to check in. When we got to the ticket counter they informed me that our flight was going to be delayed for 12 hours and would not depart until midnight. They had tried to notify us over the last couple of days by leaving messages at our hotel in Orlando, but we had checked out and spent the last two nights at my brother's in the Tampa area. This was in an age before smart phones, emails and texts when gaps in communication were the norm. My heart just sank and I was thinking what the heck am I going to do now? I was exhausted from the last ten days of travel and being solely in charge of four young children. Any parent out there can relate that sometimes when you come back from a vacation you need a vacation to recover from it.

So I thought it through and decided to go back and get another rental car. We certainly weren't going to sit in an airport for twelve hours—someone might not survive. But when we went back to the rental counter, the agent pointed out that my driver's license had expired a couple months ago— a point of detail that had escaped me considering all that had gone on in recent months. She said she couldn't rent me a car with an expired license. I asked to speak to a manager and told him the situation, including that they had just rented me a car the last ten days with an expired license, and all I was asking for to use a vehicle for less than half a day. With latitude I doubt he'd have in today's security driven world, he reasonably approved the rental despite the expiration issue. Otherwise, I don't know what Plan B would have been.

Once we were all aboard the new rental, we headed over to the east coast to Cocoa Beach where the kids could do some boogie boarding in the Atlantic. We also searched out the famous Ron Jon's Surf Shop since we had been seeing those t-shirts all week.

After a few hours of salty, sandy fun in the ocean, we moved on to Kennedy Space Center, just up the road at Cape Canaveral, for a fascinating inside look at the space program and an up close view of several massive machines that had been to Earth orbit and back. If you've ever imagined being an astronaut, a tour of this incredible facility certainly helps you visualize that dream more clearly.

Afterwards, we stopped by a local parish to catch a late Saturday evening Mass, knowing that after getting home at around 2 o'clock the next morning nobody would be in good enough shape to attend the Sunday morning service. We did all of that and turned layover lemons into lemonade and had an unexpected bonus and very memorable day. Somehow I got my second wind, and it was another affirmation of "We are the Georges! We can't be beat!"

During the trip and after we got back, I worked very hard to be patient and tolerant with the kids, knowing they would be processing their loss. So when they teased one another or tangled up in the occasional sibling scuffle, I wouldn't over react. The same went for someone not completing a chore or other responsibility. While there was a temporary "grace period" when normal discipline measures were put on hold, I knew that it couldn't go on indefinitely because I would never be able to fulfill my promises and the dreams that Linda and I shared regarding the raising of our children.

As the end of the school year and summer vacation approached, I knew that the change of rhythm and relative freedom that comes with summer break would make enforcing family rules more challenging. So in June I announced that the common courtesies and the boundaries that were part of discipline and respect for one another were back in order. I explained that what had been allowed over the last few months had been temporary, and moving forward we needed to get back to a disciplined and respectful condition. It didn't mean the wooden spoon and soap that Mom had used on rare occasions back when someone talked back or said something that was disrespectful or foul and required correction (though, sometimes I wonder if that was something I should have kept in place) but it meant that we were going to maintain order and reasonable boundaries of conduct.

The first time I needed to reel in a situation was when my daughter continued disrupting one of her brothers without letup. I got her attention and told her to go up to her room to think about what she was doing wrong. Of course, she didn't want to go up to her room, but I insisted and didn't back down. She stomped her way up the stairs and as she got to the top she turned, looked down at me and said, "I wish you had died and not Mom."

At that moment my tired mind flashed through scenes of a late night clean up of a sick little girl, mountains of laundry, helping with homework assignments , grocery runs with a tribe of kids on my heels, arranging dinners for a party of five each night—all the struggles of running a household, squeezing in my job, and getting very little sleep. How I didn't respond with, "Why you little brat!" I can't quite say. But instead, surely guided by Linda's spirit, I responded with, "Lynn, I wish Mom didn't die either."

Truthfully, I'm not that good under pressure, and I have no way to explain what came out of my mouth other than to credit divine intervention. Though the outburst was hurtful, I'm thankful that I quickly realized what she was really saying. And it was good that she expressed her pain.

But that wasn't what was really really bad.

Dianthus caryophyllus

Purple Carnation

Changeable Unreliability

7

LOOKING FOR MY HAZEL

In the mid-sixties there was a popular TV series called Hazel. Hazel was played by Shirley Booth. She was the maid for Mr. Baxter, or as she referred to him, Mr. B. While it wasn't the sixties and I wasn't necessarily looking for a maid, I did need a support person. Before Linda passed we had talked about options in this regard. One was my wonderful godmother, my Aunt Teresa. She was a beautiful soul. She was very patient and loving. She had already raised her own five children with only one adult child remaining at home. She had no husband but was grandma to a number of children that lived near her. Aunt Teresa lived about an hour away from me. She would have been perfect. I knew her, I loved her and she could be trusted. But it would have meant quitting her job which was steady employment with a Catholic operation just down the road from where she lived. It also meant her remaining son would be on his own, and it would have removed her from easy access for her other children and grandchildren, whom she cherished dearly. After thinking it through, we decided against disrupting her life and family. We also thought seriously about an au pair, thinking the cultural exchange would be a plus, but upon further research we decided that with limited work visas it would be disruptive to replace someone every time a visa waiver would run its term. In the end we settled on doing it the hard way and finding someone yet to be known by us to fill the position.

We needed an adult with experience to be there when the kids got home from school. We needed someone that could make dinners, as I was perfectly capable of handling the breakfasts and lunches. We needed someone that could do some light house work. I would handle all the kids' school related activities, the grocery shopping and the laundry.

I'll never forget the red folder my oldest son used to bring home each month. That became my scheduling bible; it was my playbook. As soon as I received it, I transcribed into my daily planner every fieldtrip, parent teacher meeting, scout meeting, hot lunch schedule, due dates for fees, and every special church activity that involved one of the kids. I did this for all four children for the next eight elementary school years. It was very important for me not to miss a school responsibility as I never wanted them to be embarrassed for being delinquent as a no show, or not having papers signed or forgetting field trip money and the like. There were to be no excuses on my part because I was flying solo. Also, I felt it was very important to set a good example and avoid modeling a life of easy excuses for my children.

The heavily filled schedule also included everyone's extracurricular activities. Throughout raising them I strongly encouraged extracurricular involvement whether it was in sports, art, dance or music. I never wanted them to bow out of opportunities by leaning on the excuse of only having one parent.

If they had an interest and would follow though each season, I would support their interest—no time for excuses.

Over the years, the list of interests included football, basketball, volleyball, soccer, little league, softball, track, cross country, karate, skiing, dance, piano and, I'm sure, some that I have forgotten. But for each of the four children I had a ready yes for whatever interested them and made sure we never missed a registration deadline.

As far as laundry and grocery shopping were concerned, I could do those things at off hours. Laundry in particular could be done any time. And with four active kids, there was plenty of laundry to do. In fact, at one point I called a family meeting to talk about laundry—specifically the use of towels. I had found that some people were taking a shower and then tossing the fresh towel they'd just used right into the hamper because it was easier than hanging it up. So I said, "Let me get this straight. You have just taken a shower; your body is clean and you take a clean towel to dry off a clean body, and then you put it in the hamper?"

Perhaps they'd picked this up from our hotel stay in Florida, but I made it clear that I wasn't in the hotel laundry business, and that I needed everyone's help to keep the laundry monster under control. From that point on towels were reused for a week before they made it into the dirty laundry pile.

In my role as Lord of the Laundry, I discovered the best time to process our never-ending supply of dirty clothes, towels and linens was late at night and into the early morning. Like a factory worker, I would shift loads from washer to dryer to baskets, keeping the line moving until the last load finally was tumbling away inside the dryer. Usually, that last load was ready to take out in the morning—having turned the dryer back on for an extra ten minutes to take the wrinkles out. Then I would fold it up or locate an item if someone needed something particular for school that day.

Some men are intimidated by the task of doing the laundry with all those dials and push-pull elements, not to mention all the rules about sorting and colors. But I have to say that the degree of difficulty is overestimated in most cases. As long as you separate something dark or new that might bleed the first time it is washed, are careful with the items requiring special handling, and separate the whites from the darks, all should be fine. I don't recall ruining lots of clothes in the washing process—maybe just a few unintended streaks of extra color and an inadvertent size reduction here and there.

Off hours for grocery shopping was also the rule. I would get the bulk of the week's groceries at the market on Sunday at 6:30 a.m., while the kids were sleeping. I found the store to be nearly empty of customers and all the shelves restocked from the night before, making the items on my list quick and easy to find. I first started grocery shopping while in college when Linda and I married my junior year. She had a fulltime job and I was a fulltime student—which hardly consumed the 40-plus hours her job required—so I had more time to get what little groceries we needed. Since I was familiar with comparing pricing and choosing products, I continued to shop for groceries after we started our family. Besides being necessary, it was an opportunity to give her a break and a bit of quiet time, so I would take the kids with me to do the shopping in the early years of raising our family. Of course, taking the kids along meant that it took twice as long, because in addition to finding what we needed, I always had to fend off multiple suggestions and pleas for items that weren't on the list.

The job description for my version of Hazel was to provide dinners, be there when the kids were home from school, and to keep up with some light house work, while leaving some chores for the kids to participate in. I felt that the work load would be reasonable for the right person. And as I had placed ads in several area publications, I was confident of getting the assistance I needed. As summer vacation approached, I especially needed someone to stand guard, because school wasn't there to occupy the children.

One of the first responses I received came as a result of someone who knew our story and passed on the ad on to a friend. This friend had qualified a person with specific experience that would match nicely with what we needed. She was from the area in which we lived, familiar with the community and had worked with a family the previous 17 years helping a gentleman raise his four children, with the youngest in college now and their needs fulfilled. She had been an administrator with the PTA, involved in scouting and generally well networked. She seemed almost heaven sent, I felt, as if Linda had guided her to us.

This individual needed a place to stay as well, so she moved into our fifth room office that was converted into a bedroom. This was a plus since she would be available during off hours if I had a work requirement. She spent her weekends with family that lived about two hours away. I felt as though this arrangement was a winner. By all appearances it seemed to be exactly what the doctor ordered.

When someone moves into your home and becomes part of the rhythm of the household, there definitely is a transition period. I was willing to step back, observe and be patient, and I encouraged my children, especially the older ones, to do the same. I saw the younger two quickly migrate to this woman. After all, she represented the mother figure. I remember seeing my daughter holding on to her leg as they stood together. They were looking to her to fill the huge void left in their mother's absence, if only for a little bit and a little while.

After the first month, I heard some murmuring that this person was mean or would yell at them or shoo them away with a kick. Being very careful not to overreact to children still making a transition to someone new and getting used to someone other than their mother for the first time, I also cautioned them and tried to help them understand what it might take for someone to be in her position. But it was a challenge to communicate to four different children with a seven year age range and have them all understand. So after my attempts to enlighten them, I let more time pass and kept an eye on the situation. I definitely wanted this need solved, but I certainly would not tolerate unacceptable behavior.

More time passed and I would occasionally walk with the kids around the neighborhood in the evening when I returned from work to allow them to share or sometimes vent about what had transpired earlier in the day. After a few months of remaining patient and fostering this new relationship, it was becoming clear that while this person had the right resume, she was now in her mid fifties and was losing the patience needed for another round of raising a family at this stage in her life. This was totally understandable. Although I'm a bit older than she was then, I too would have a tough time mustering the energy and enthusiasm, not to mention the patience, in starting all over again with a new family and having day in and day out responsibilities and challenges. It truly was a lot to ask.

The tipping point came over an issue that wasn't related to her interpersonal skills. She took the boys to a barber and got them all buzz cuts. The buzz cut was not in vogue back then as it is today and it really shocked and dismayed me when I first saw them. I felt that she had made a serious personal decision without consulting me. I'm sure she meant well, but I felt she over stepped her bounds. The boys, particularly the older two, felt helpless and humiliated. We parted ways shortly thereafter, mutually agreeing that the relationship was not a healthy or productive one. I decided to end it immediately without lining up a replacement. I didn't want to risk anymore shocks or surprises.

That meant I needed to fill for a few weeks, so I covered the best I could, which simply meant less sleep. I ran some more ads and talked to my network of friends putting the word out that I needed Hazel number 2. When a friend recommended someone that they knew through the local YMCA who was in her early twenties, it instantly sounded like someone I should interview.

She was young, which meant more energy and less chance of burn out, and she had a part time position at the YMCA, which suggested she had a recreational advantage which would be good for creating activities for my 5 and 7 year old. This was especially important because we still had half of the summer vacation to fill.

After interviewing several candidates, I selected the young lady with the YMCA experience. Unlike our first support person, she did not need to stay with us and only reported Monday through Friday during the day while I was at work. It was game on again with great hopes that this would be the winner where I could depend on this new support person and hopefully be able to continue to balance the attention required at my job with keeping the family safe and well cared for.

Things were actually moving along very well at work. We had changed the music format 18 months before. Although Classic Rock Hits has become a mainstay genre format a quarter century later, back then our station was one of the very first in the country to introduce it. I was fortunate to have superior support and dependability from someone who doubled as the morning show co-host and Operations Director, a gentleman by the name of Dave, who still occupies that position today. He was a talent that I could always count on. His attention to product quality control allowed me the flexibility to balance the demands I was facing in my career and on the home front.

Work was going so well that for the first time I qualified for the annual bonus paid out based on bottom line performance. I had special plans for that bonus that I hoped would serve as a real positive in the kids' lives. It would be something for them to anticipate, all the while distracting them, if ever so little, from the tragedy they had just lived though earlier in the year. It related to something their mother promised them the year before: that once everyone learned to swim (the younger two were completing their certification that summer) we would get a pool. I think she had in mind an above ground pool, but I was determined to do a little better than that. Acknowledging that I could never replace what they lost, I still strived to do my best for them. In this case, it meant getting an in ground pool. I hoped the anticipation of future fun would occupy their thoughts. The steam shovel excavating to start the project off in the back yard was a nice distraction. And then a couple months of following the build out progress was going to help get us through summer and the next school year.

Hazel number two was also short lived lasting only two months. In the first month I recognized some behavior that I thought was questionable but I couldn't confirm. In the meantime, the kids were adjusting to her and growing to like her, once again forming an attachment because she was filling that mother figure role in their lives.

But one day I arrived home an hour early and found her standing on the front stoop of the house. She was swaying ever so slightly. As I approached, I could see that her eyes were bloodshot and I could smell that she had been drinking. I called her mother to come and pick her up. That was the last we ever saw of her.

Shortly thereafter I learned that she was a recovering alcoholic. No one bothered to warn me. Here she was overseeing the care and transportation of four children, sometimes also including neighbor kids in a carpool, and no one thought that it may be dangerous enough to give me a heads up about her problem. It also came out that earlier on her last day my younger two were at a birthday party up the hill a few blocks away, and on the way home my youngest had pulled open the sliding door of the minivan while they were moving, and she had been completely oblivious to it.

Once I explained to the kids her status as no longer being with us, they began to recall how sometimes she went off the road onto the shoulder, just thinking she was a bad driver. In retrospect it's clear that we dodged a number of bullets during those dangerous two months and that the family's guardian angel was working overtime.

It seemed like I just couldn't get it right. I ran another ad in the local paper and put the word out that I was looking for Hazel number 3. I was on the phone talking to a friend who also was a customer of the station. He asked how I was doing and I mentioned that I was back in the market looking for a support person. He mentioned someone that he was very familiar with who had just gone through a divorce and who was looking for something to fill her days. At this time I had not yet received any responses to my ad, so I decided to interview the candidate my friend recommended.

It was a very good interview. She was personable and impeccably dressed. She lived in the area and didn't require moving into our converted room. She was recently divorced, and an experienced mother with a son the same age as my second oldest son. She seemed more than capable of making dinners, doing some light housework and being dependably there when the kids would come home from school, as now the new school year was just beginning. We quickly agreed upon the compensation and she started that next Monday after I had introduced her to the kids.

Hazel number 3 started out as a delight, and a bonus was that she was good at doing craft activities. At Halloween and at Thanksgiving she provided a nice touch with decorations and created an atmosphere of fun. At this time the children were in kindergarten, first grade, fifth grade and eighth grade. I felt the creative, crafty aspect she brought was especially nice for the younger two; it was something Mom would have done with them, so it was a bonus offering from the support person position. Also about this time the pool installation was coming to completion, so even though we were into September, the in-pool heater allowed us to use it into the early fall and gave the kids a bit of fun then, with something fun to anticipate over the cold, snowy winter. The anticipation of more splashing and swimming in the coming year brightened their winter, if only a little bit, as we were trying to get more days in between Mom's passing and the next day to lighten that weight that still hung over our family.

I noticed that Hazel number 3 came somewhat over-dressed everyday, looking like she did on her interview. I often wondered how she handled the housework being dressed so nicely. She would arrive in the afternoon while the kids were still in school, do some housework, make dinner and be there when the school bus dropped the kids off. It all seemed to be coming together. I thought we finally had someone that was right for our situation. The kids liked her and, once again, the younger ones were beginning to form an attachment to her.

After the first six weeks or so I wanted to discuss how it was working out for her, hoping that she was feeling as positive as I was. Rather than discuss things at the house around the kids, we arranged to meet at a local restaurant in a neutral place where she could talk freely without the kids overhearing the conversation, in case there were issues. We talked and everything seemed to be good with her. I was relieved and felt that finally we had found the one.

It was a few days after that meeting that she come back to the house late one evening to pick something up. The kids were already in bed. It was my laundry night so I was up tending to that. It turned out that she just wanted someone to talk to as lingering issues from her divorce were unsettling her. So I listened and tried to console her with words as best I could not knowing all of the details. Just before leaving she asked me for a hug. Naively I obliged, thinking nothing of it. But over the next couple of weeks it became increasingly uncomfortable for me. She wanted more hugs and wanted to go away from the house to meet and talk about the kids. But when I asked if there were any problems, she indicated that there were not.

I was starting to catch on that she had mistaken that initial meeting at the restaurant as a date. So I suggested we just close the doors to the dining room and meet there. She said some other suggestive things to me which finally clued me in that she really wanted more than a job; she was interested in having a relationship.

As this realization hit me, I became rather upset. I was heavily disappointed. I thought I'd finally reached the goal of finding the right caregiver for my family so I could get back to focusing on work and providing for them. But now her actions were making things awkward and complicated. Linda had passed only six months earlier and I was not even close to moving on. I was upset because this was a job for which I was paying her a fair amount, but for her it was about her designs on me.

It finally got so uncomfortable that just after the New Year I terminated our arrangement. The children, especially the younger two, were once again dangerously attaching themselves to their caregiver, and knowing this situation wasn't going to continue, I decided to make a change. As hard as it was to accept, once again I had to find another support person.

Afterwards, the kids pointed out to me that there were the many times she would play The Sound Of Music on the VCR for the kids to watch. The famous story line there, of course, is where the very proper nanny, played by Julie Andrews, is placed with the Von Trapp family: a widower (played by Christopher Plummer) and his children. The story ends with the nanny marrying Mr. Von Trapp, and they all become one big happy family. I guess I should have seen this coming, but it was new territory for me.

Hazel number 4 was found a result of widening our net. I decided to run ads outside of the area including the Fox Valley. There was a very promising response that came from the Green Bay area. This time I took the older two boys with me to get their opinion. I was 0 for 3 so far and could use some screening assistance it seemed.

The candidate was delightful albeit a bit more gruff than we expected. But we needed somebody and the two older boys' first impression was positive enough for us to come to terms with her. She was going to stay with us in the extra room but only during the week. She would head back to Green Bay most weekends. There were no special craft skills with this support person, in fact she'd never had any children or experience with them. Although she was somewhere in her mid to late twenties, she didn't necessarily have an abundance of energy. But she was dependable and adequate when it came to housework. Her cooking was acceptable, especially as we were generally easy to please. Linda and I never allowed our kids to be picky eaters. I was raised in a family of ten where being "picky" just wasn't an option.

I didn't, however, have full confidence that she would be around for very long. She admitted that she took the job because she needed the money. She had lost her job just prior to responding to our advertisement. She didn't have any special affinity for kids, but she was more kind than not. Yet, I always sensed the four hour round trip home and back each week was a hardship for her.

Here we were, just about a year down the road from Linda's funeral, and we were already into our fourth Hazel figure, with possibly a fifth just around the corner. Each time the kids bought into the hope that this was going to be our future. And each time the kids tried to fill their own void and form an attachment to the closest thing representing a mother figure in their lives. It was hard to watch. While I had tried my best, and actually had experience in screening and hiring people as part of my career responsibility, with an excellent record of success there, I was failing miserably at filling this all important position. Like before, there was no handbook or YouTube video to guide me.

Over that last year, in an attempt to find the right caregiver for my family, I had brought in a person who was impatient and mean, a recovering alcoholic with incredibly bad judgment, someone who had ulterior motives in pushing for a relationship with me, and lastly, someone that had short term plans who was there for the paycheck and not necessarily for the kids. This aspect of our year of transition was a disaster in my eyes. The only good thing was that a whole year was now in between Linda's passing and the current day.

But that wasn't what was really really bad.

Lilium concolor

SCARLET LILY

Aspiration

8

IN PURSUIT OF STABILITY

It had been a little over a year since Linda passed away and almost two and a half years since she was diagnosed with cancer. To say that I still really missed her would be an understatement. In spite of the kids keeping me busy with their needs, I was starting to feel lonely. I missed her companionship, the partnership we shared raising our family, her love. I missed her and everything she meant to me. I found Sundays to be especially hard. It was the day we typically went to church and spent time together as part of weekend free time. I remember hearing the kids playing outside and just laying back on the top of the stairs on the second level and just crying. I cried often when I was alone in the car. I never wanted them to see me because I felt a responsibility to be the strong one, and if they saw me break down it would make them nervous that everything wasn't going to be alright; and I had to make it ALL right. It was up to me and only me. I couldn't expose my weakness.

I knew the year of transition was going to be a challenge as is the first year of any new endeavor either personal or business. I expected that there would be growing pains but I just didn't think it would be so difficult to establish some stability and continuity in my effort of finding a support person. But I should have guessed that finding someone—even on a paid basis —who could come in and mesh with a family of five and demonstrate even a fraction of the concern and devotion as someone biologically attached was probably asking too much. A family of four kids is considered above average size, and it generates a lot of work and stress.

I had adjusted to the above average size of my family; after all, they were mine. It was my life and coming from a family of eight kids made it feel relatively manageable by comparison. But even after this hard lesson, I still had plenty to learn in my expectations of partnering up with someone new and having it work.

Working hard to recruit, hire, orient and adjust to a new caregiver, then dealing with the overwhelming frustration and disappointment when things didn't work out had taken its toll. After terrible failures, I lost all confidence in my ability to find the right person. Old, young, tolerant, strict; I really was at a loss. I knew my margin for error was now zero. I dreaded the thought of putting my family on yet another emotional rollercoaster. This was only compounding the loss of their mother.

I felt more vulnerable than I ever had before. Then, right around that time, I met a social worker from Children's Service Society. We were introduced in the hallway at my radio station by our News Director in charge of Public Service. The social worker was there to be interviewed for our Sunday morning public service show. She had and omnipresent smile and was pleasingly attractive to the eye. I followed up with her the next day to discuss her experience with our radio operation while at the same time trying to determine if I wanted to take the conversation in a personal direction. And that is where it naturally led. She had a wonderful background in social work, which I'm sure was part of the attraction. She had a splendid sense of humor. She had never been married. In fact, up to that point she hadn't been in any relationship for more than a month or two, which meant she had no former relationship baggage. She had a daughter a year older than my daughter. She was a devout Catholic which was important to me, especially as at the time as I was still raising my children. And best of all, she was available and surprisingly seemed interested in me. We initiated a whirlwind courtship.

After six weeks of dating we got engaged. In fact, I proposed from the radio station's hot air balloon as we flew about fifteen hundred feet over the house where I lived. It was important to her that she get engaged before her 30th birthday, which was coming up the next week. We were married eight weeks later. If you're doing the math, that would be 98 days from the day we met to the day we married. It sounds absolutely crazy now (it actually sounded really crazy many years ago, too) but it didn't feel so crazy while it was happening. Was I in a desperate place and unaware of it? But to marry this available and good person meant that my stability problems would be solved. Marry someone and life becomes dependable, with no more rotating Hazels and no more kids getting attached and detached. I had been in a beautiful relationship with Linda for twenty years. I knew the formula: be kind, patient, understanding and willing to compromise. Put your wife first and live by the pledge "till death do us part." I thought all my problems were solved, but actually, they were about to go from bad to worse.

As one might guess, the marriage was a challenge from the beginning. It had only been 15 months since I lost my wife, and my children their mother. Now we were blending families. I was cautioned that as a social worker, it would be natural that my new wife may be on a rescue mission and not even realize it. We talked about that being a possible attraction and after our discussion we both felt fine that rescuing my family was not the emphasis. Still, her background as a social worker had played a part in our expanding family. Besides my four children and her daughter, within a very short time we became a foster home to two beautiful little girls that were 2 and 4 years old. Their mother was incarcerated and actually had five children by four different fathers. We also temporarily took on an infant on a part time basis who had been born to a mother hooked on cocaine. And if that wasn't enough, we took in my nephew from Florida. He was headed in bad places, so my sister and her husband asked if our household might offer him a positive influence. Of course, my new wife highly endorsed that we assist. We accepted and he moved in. Little did anyone know that we too were soon to be headed in bad places.

So we only knew each other for three months before marrying, we were blending my four children with her daughter, we took in two displaced toddlers, plus we welcomed a nephew in need of boundaries and guidance, and we also occasionally cared for a cocaine baby. And we couldn't make it work—go figure!

My explanation to my children upon each expansion was that we had the love and the resources, so it was something we were called to do. To whom much is given, much is expected. But it clearly was an overreach. The stress on the family was overwhelming. Part of my accepting the expansion was to please my new wife, after all, she was going to be making significant contributions in partnering with me to raise my children. I wanted her to be fulfilled. Of her own volition, she resigned her job, which she was happy to do, because now for the first time she could be a stay at home mom for her daughter, not having to work for financial reasons. So in the spirit of helping her feel fulfilled and to keep her connected with her history of social work we opened our house to foster the growth of others as well.

In addition, at that time I found myself stretching thin with community service commitments. I served as a volunteer on the Board of Directors for Children's Service Society, was a Vice President for the Leukemia Society, and managed a number of groups at our local parish including the Altar Servers, managed the marketing and promotion for the church festival, and ran the meal program that the church sponsored. That service in particular I felt was most beneficial as I also involved my children in the serving of the meals to those in need. I felt that it was a wonderful reality check compared to the somewhat privileged life they enjoyed.

In retrospect, I can see that I was crowding my schedule to distract me from the sadness of the monumental loss of my best friend, and trying to stay so busy I didn't have time to dwell on that loss.

It should be no surprise, then, that with everything on our plate, we didn't give our core relationship the focus and priority it needed to develop. One of the obstacles I know she faced was that she was always following the ghost of Linda and the unknown. I was quite aware of this potential and was very conscious of not talking to her about things Linda and I did or said. I wanted this to be a new beginning for both of us.

Despite many sessions with therapist professionals (which I could just feel shaking their heads as they learned our story) we were unable to make the relationship and family blend without great stress. My wife would become overwhelmed and I still can picture her announcing to us as I was preparing breakfast and making lunches for school that she was leaving. Sometimes it was for days, sometimes for weeks, and then sometimes for whole months. I can still picture my daughter's face with tears streaming down; she had become so attached once again. And every time a departure was announced, I was left with my four children, two foster kids, and my troubled nephew. I was going backwards very fast. But it was the tears and disruption of my younger two children that really got my attention. With no success resulting from the family therapy sessions I decided I needed to file for divorce and stop the insanity. It was an incredibly hard decision. I remember early on the different times she had left. I remember sitting up at night looking out my bedroom with the window open, hoping that the sound of each car that came up the street was surely her returning. And then when an occasional car would slow and turn up our block I got even more excited because it had to be her. But it never was.

It was very hard to accept all of this. With Linda it was death. It was final. It could not be reversed. There is nothing that can be done. You have to accept it. But in this situation this person still walks the earth. Surely this can be remedied. There had to be a solution; because I could touch it and it could breathe it could be fixed. Conflicts could be solved. It was a very male like attitude. But I also learned in the therapy sessions that you can only work on yourself; you can't work on anyone else. That is for them to acknowledge and address.

My wife had never been in any significant relationship up to the time I met her. And now she was not interested or available to stay in the marriage we were in. Still, she wrote to me saying that she wanted to stay married, but she also couldn't stay in the marriage. It actually got me to withdraw the divorce decree that was filed in 1990. But within the next year, nothing had changed, and all I was doing was confusing my children, thinking there was hope for this person fulfilling the idea of her being their mother, but only hurting them with her absence from the marriage and the household. So, once again, I filed for divorce and this time I did not withdraw my petition. It was an amicable divorce: not complicated primarily because there were no biological children involved and also because the courts regarded it as a short term marriage.

Getting a divorce was against everything I believed in up until that time. When I heard of someone headed to divorce, I looked at them as being weak, uncommitted and as being a promise breaker. It simply was not acceptable as I was very judgmental. But like most things, until you walk in someone's shoes, you really can't judge them. I never imagined that I would be party to a divorce. The day of the divorce proceedings, my soon-to-be ex-wife didn't even appear at the court house. Instead, the judge contacted her at work, introduced himself and put her on the speaker phone so she could not only witness the hearing but also have the opportunity to comment and/or ask questions about the proceedings, understanding that it was soon to be final based on the powers of the court. The hearing was brief with no comment offered on her part. The settlement was reasonable and fair to both parties and had been agreed upon prior to the court date.

This hearing was almost a year and a half since I filed the second petition. Courts move slow with enforced waiting periods and many other cases to hear. As the judge signed the final decree, the irony of the date hit me with full force. This divorce was granted by the court on March 11—the same day that Linda passed away five years earlier.

But that wasn't what was really really bad.

Geranium platypetalum

GERANIUM

Determination

9

IF AT FIRST YOU DON'T SUCCEED

Marriage wasn't as simple as I remembered it. When I met Linda at 14, it was love at first sight. We dated though our teen years— when adolescents typically change and outgrow each other during the formative years—and we weathered that together. Then we handled the early years of raising four babies through infancy and toddlerhood and survived that. It seemed the only issues we had any differences of opinion on had to do with decisions involving the children.

Most parents can relate to that dynamic: both partners sharing the goal of raising well adjusted human beings. Of course, planning the best route to that destination is always subject to debate. But we were lucky in that we agreed on the major issues in raising our children. When they were younger and Linda was a full time mom, she put in place a code of consequences to help manage their behavior. When they would sass back, say unacceptable things or tease one another to cause fights, she wielded a wooden spoon on their bottoms and a bar of soap that cleaned their mouths when they used inappropriate language. Both the spoon and soap stood by mostly as deterrent props, but they served as important reminders of the law of consequences. However, when Linda was no longer with us, those items were not adopted into my disciplinary arsenal. Based on my compassion for their loss, I opted for more lenient responses to misconduct that occurred in the early days without their mother.

After going through multiple caregivers and then a failed marriage, I should have realized it was going to be very tough to achieve success with our package. Adapting to the dynamics of any family would present a challenge. But with four children, it would be a lot for anyone to step in, fit in and take control, especially when there is no biological attachment or emotional interest. It's just a tough thing to do. And you can't blame the kids, just as you would not blame them when their natural parents end up in divorce. It was the reality of a package deal, and I was beginning to feel sorry for the hand I had been dealt. Linda was more right than she realized. In her final taped message to me she had predicted that life was going to be very very tough as a single parent. But I can honestly say I never got jealous of Linda's peace or mad at God's decisions. Then again, according to the steps of grieving, I probably needed to.

It was the spring of 1992. By the time of the official termination of my second marriage, we had been separated for most of the two previous years. So what I did during that, starting with the separation period, was find someone that was available to meet the kids around 3 p.m. when they got home from school and make us dinner, leaving by about 6 p.m. as I would arrive home from work. This system seemed to mitigate the emotional attachment and inevitable disappointment, and it served the essential needs of the household, figuring that I would handle the rest. We actually had a pretty good run at that.

But the smooth run came to an end when one particular caregiver, who was also widowed, wanted to develop our involvement beyond the business relationship it was meant to be. I was not interested. She even went out of her way to win over the kids. She let my 15 year old son drive her hot new Z28 on occasion, despite the fact that he was not licensed. A neighbor discretely alerted me that this was going on after she saw him driving past her house. In as kind but firm terms as I knew how, I made it clear to her that I had no personal interest. She was a very nice and kind person, but I simply wanted and needed the arrangement we had initially agreed upon. Soon after that she gave up and left, and I was looking for another candidate … again. It seemed the search was a never ending revolving door.

As the last couple of years I was essentially companion free, and with the recent marriage failure, I was determined to move on for a number of reasons. First, my youngest son was 10 and my daughter 12 years old by now. They were young enough that I felt they still needed a maternal figure in their lives to complete their balanced growth. And especially as my daughter was reaching the age of womanhood, I thought it was important for her to have a mother figure for guidance. It is what I felt at the time, but time would prove that all my concerns in trying to do what I thought was the right thing then weren't necessary. I certainly didn't want to go back to the route of finding a support person. My failure there was still fresh in my mind. And I took the failed marriage personally, so I was bound and determined to prove that I was a good husband, that I was marriage worthy. It is something I always strongly believed in and being married, sharing your life, your ups and your downs with someone significant in your life was an important state that I always desired to be in. It essentially had been my life since I was 14 years old. It was something I felt I did well looking back on my 20 years with Linda.

So I made a conscious effort to move forward and give attention to my happiness as well, cognizant that there would only be limited acceptance from the kids in this regard. I would be in the middle no matter what. More importantly, I still felt there was time to become whole as a family again and an individual, so I opened myself up to another relationship.

It would be an understatement to say I would have been a perfect case study as a candidate for a rebound marriage. In late spring I met someone on a business call and as we talked we realized we had previously lived in the same neighborhood at one time, but had never met. She was aware of me and had bumped into Linda in local retail markets and commented what a pretty and nice woman she was.

This innocent comment sharpened my insight about the biggest obstacle in my recently failed marriage: my partner's feeling that she was dealing with an unknown. She had heard all the wonderful things about Linda and felt she was expected to live up to an impossible standard; continually walking in Linda's tall, glowing shadow. Despite my sensitivity and reassurances on the issue, her paranoia persisted. There was nothing I could do to counter her feelings about it. So when I heard that this new person had known Linda and knew our story it was a relief.

People try to make sure the problem that existed in a previous relationship is one of the first things you look to satisfy in the next. It is human nature to not want to get into something that you just spent the last few years battling to get around. Foolishly though, sometimes if that one problem area doesn't exist, you don't notice anything else and even rationalize issues that you know will bring trouble; just as long as the one big concern from last time is absent from the new relationship.

We dated over the next year. She made it clear she was not expecting for us to just be dating for too long a period and that marriage was important to her. She had been married twice before, both times ending in divorce, but it was still important to her that a commitment was forthcoming. Of course, the two divorce history did not register a double red flag with me at the time. It can be said now, probably in a slightly arrogant way, that I felt her previous marriages didn't work because she hadn't met a man like me, who through life had developed some sensitivities and compassion, and who had what it took to make a marriage work. It would seem that I gave myself too much credit.

In June of 1993, my mother passed away relatively unexpectedly at just 65 years of age. She had raised eight children, a large family by any standard. Though it had been her choice, she had also been handicapped, in a sense, by never learning to drive. She was more or less a captive in her own house with eight kids and no easy escape. She was a good mother in that her children were kept safe, fed, neat and clean. But she did occasionally lose her patience; fairly understandable considering the crowd of little people all in such a close environment. I don't think any of us got especially close to her except the baby of the family, who at one point finally had her all to himself. But we all loved her and gave her the respect that parents deserve.

In my case, life was so busy once Linda and I started our family, and especially once I was flying solo, that I didn't have much occasion to connect with my mother. Of course, I always made some form of contact on birthdays, anniversaries, holidays and other special occasions and some contact at other times. She was especially helpful in keeping me informed about the ways I could help my parents over the years. She would share details of certain needs which my father would not be comfortable discussing with me. This allowed me to assist them in a number of ways that otherwise I might never have discovered. So when she passed at a relatively young age, it made me think about life and reminded me how fragile and brief it is with no guaranteed end date. Her death prompted me into an engagement to marry again the week after her passing. I was reminded of my own mortality and the need to move forward in life. Plus, I was looking once again to make my family whole, find a partner for companionship and create a stable environment where I could depend on someone to be there consistently after school, provide meals and help out with the operation of the household. But mostly I desired the sense of stability that I had been chasing over the last seven years.

Four months after our engagement we married. Like before, the blended family challenges were instantly manifested. Having some recent experience to draw upon, I was somewhat conditioned and it didn't blindside me; I knew what it looked like. She also had two sons: one getting married and one in senior high school. While neither one lived in our household, there was still the merging and sharing aspect and a new dynamic created in the effort of blending families. It can't be argued that I moved too fast in trying to make my family whole. I wasn't patient enough and didn't take the proper time to get to know this new person fully. I do take full responsibility. We dated about a year and a half before we married, yet even that wasn't enough time. Of course, relative to the 98 days from introduction to vows in my last marriage, it seemed like a reasonable amount of time by comparison. But I was applying pretzel logic. It wasn't long before I realized my lack of patience in choosing wisely had put me on another track to failure.

The blending challenges and the personality conflicts with the kids continued to put me in the middle. I always stressed with my kids how a marriage is primary and must come first. It was a lesson I wanted them to take into their future marriages and probably the most important thing I could teach them. But there were times I just couldn't defend my spouse's actions or the unaccountable periods of time when she was unreachable, especially when I would need her to pick or drop someone off from school or extracurricular events. Within the first year or two there were many very vocal arguments. It was when a couple of the arguments ended in her telling me how she was going to take me for everything I had in settlement that I started to look seriously at the disingenuous nature of the relationship . They say sometimes the truth comes out in anger. Coupled with the history of her previous litigations that she had shared with me, I came to believe her threats of leaving with a big settlement in tow to be true. It wasn't long afterwards that I filed a petition for divorce. Even after experiencing it, divorce was still a foreign concept to me, and while the decision did not come easy, it was easier this time. But just like before, I withdrew my petition, wanting to make sure I was doing the right thing.

It wasn't long, though, before I once again heard how she was going to "spank" me in a settlement and go after as much as she could get. This from a woman who essentially brought nothing material to the marriage and who wanted to dig into my worth and years of hard work, none of which she'd been present for in supporting my efforts to obtain. Still, I took her very seriously because of what I had learned of her past settlements. So I moved forward with a petition for divorce because I was counseled that the best way to fend off her threats was to see that it would be a short term marriage.

I had always dreamed about marrying my high school sweetheart, the love of my life, and living happily ever after. Instead I lost my best friend and the mother of my children to cancer, and I'd been divorced not once, but twice in less than ten years!

But that isn't what was really really bad

.

Hedera helix

IVY

Endurance

10

GRADUATIONS AND AN ACCIDENT

In March of 1997 it had been 10 years since Linda had passed away. A lot had transpired as we fought our way forward in our effort to move on. Being a person of continual optimism, always believing that problems can be solved, I pride myself in looking for the silver lining. I believe it is there, even though it is not always obvious while we live out our experiences. As I reflected on the last decade, it became obvious to me that the nearly nonstop parade of disruption we faced had been a huge distraction from the major tragedy that hit our family. That, of course, wasn't the master plan but it's just the way it happened.

My intention then was to take my four children away on the tenth year anniversary and go some place fun to celebrate moving forward and the fact that we were all still standing. We headed for a long weekend in the Grand Bahamas. We also took my oldest son's fiancé. They had been dating for about six years and they were to be married the following summer. She had always been an older sister to my daughter and had grown to be a member of our family. We toasted our survivorship recognizing that what happened to us ten years ago was already the worst thing we experienced, which helped to put our trials through the last decade in perspective.

During these years the kids were graduating from high school and from college, and by now our needs as a family had graduated as well. There was no longer a need to have a support person or a mother figure to help guide the kids. Over the next couple of years our simple need was finding someone available to provide dinners. Everything else was being handled by me or the kids as they pitched in. I was still interested in bringing balance to my life in finding a companion, but those I had dated during this time were not the answer. By 1999, the day to day needs of my family had changed significantly from 12 years earlier when we were first on our own. My oldest son had graduated from the University of Minnesota a few years earlier, had married his high school sweetheart and started his professional career working in media for a well known local television station. My second son was heading into grad school earning his Masters for Physical Therapy at the University of Wisconsin Madison. My daughter had just graduated high school and was heading off to college two hours away, while my youngest son was completing his senior year in high school. Within the next year, my two youngest would also be attending the University of Wisconsin Madison pursuing their fields of interest.

Other than my ongoing commitment to provide for their tuition, living expenses, and healthcare needs, allowing them to focus on getting good grades, my responsibilities were being reduced. Not that I was done providing for them. In fact, I kept as my goal making sure as they married, each one would have the wedding they dreamed of, and along with that I had a very ambitious goal of gifting each of them the down payment for their first house, allowing them to immediately start building equity rather than paying rent as they set out on their own with their spouses. The last dozen years were a blur of activity. But I found the time to be very liberating, and despite the failures in blending my family in marriage over the years, I felt the goals their mother and I set were accomplished for the most part, even though we had been through a lot.

Over these years there were college orientations to attend, dorm rooms and apartments on campus to be moved into. Every parent establishing their kids on campus can relate to the hauling trailers, finding a legal parking spot that would shorten the walk as you shuttled belongings to the new living quarters and waiting for your turn on the elevator as you competed with the other families moving their students in. And being the end of August it was typically hot. But these were good memories, especially knowing my kids were in well-respected higher education institutions, with the last three having ultimately received their degrees from the University of Wisconsin Madison. I know their mother would have been proud of this accomplishment as it was the educational dream we both shared, second only to the dream that if they married they would all find their perfect mate as a lifelong partner; something else as they all arrived at that stage in life that I know she would have been pleased and full of approval for the partners they were to marry.

And in helping Linda's spirit be present at those ceremonies I took advantage of making significant contributions to the local parish we belonged to as they were in the process of designing and building a new church. I decided to cover the cost for all the stained glass dormer windows in the new church thinking that as the sunlight came into the church on their special day it would represent Linda's beaming smile of approval. The church also needed to have a substantially larger piano for what was going to be a substantially larger worship area. They needed to raise $44,000 and set out to sell sponsorships at $500 by selling each of the 88 keys one at a time. After a period of time they were only able to get 12 keys sponsored, and the trial period was coming to an end; the piano would either have to be purchased or returned. Because music had been so important to Linda, I thought it was fitting to step in and take over the full sponsorship, so I dedicated the piano in Linda's name, hoping once again that her spirit, through the dedication in music and song, would be part of their future wedding ceremonies. In addition, every time we would attend Mass there we would have the same benefit of feeling her presence. I scheduled Masses in honor of Linda every year on her birth date, on Christmas, on the day she passed away and on the children's birthdays. Having the stained glass and piano dedicated in her name was going to extend her presence and memory even more.

Out of the three remaining children to marry, two of them had their wedding ceremonies at that church. When my daughter married, the sun beamed through the stained glass and shown upon her head and veil casting a glowing aura around her as she and the groom were seated at the altar area. It was a beautiful, amazing sight, and many commented on it afterwards.

The time had come for reflection on my kids' elementary and secondary education years. A flood of memories of all the activities came upon me. Playing Santa Claus each Christmas until the youngest was no longer a believer. The annual family getaways and the entertainment. Each summer we visited the local Six Flags theme park and a water park with more water rides than you could fit in one day. These trips typically allowed each one to bring a friend with them. It was a treat for their friend but also gave them someone to spend a special day with. There were annual ski trips to local hills and sometimes to the Rocky Mountains. My second son got into skiing early on and introduced the rest of us to what would become a family sport and get away. Two of my sons' passion for the activity led them to become ski patrol members. These annual trips also included an opportunity to bring a friend along. I especially enjoyed the chance to be with one or more of my children on the ski lift. We were high above ground almost touching the sky. I felt closer to God, especially as I looked at all the beauty of his creation in a glistening winter wonderland stretching out far below. Sure it was a bit cold at times, but that was part of surviving the elements which was also rewarding. Plus it provided some one-on-one time with my children which was an increasingly rare occurrence as they moved through their own busy lives.

Other entertainment over the years included many, many concerts. As a privilege of the business that I was in, I always had the opportunity to buy tickets including those to sold out events. My sons especially were sports fans so there were many Major League Baseball games, National Football League games and NBA basketball games over the years. And, of course, often times they were welcome to bring a friend. They also were privileged to enjoy behind the scenes activity in getting into the Milwaukee Brewers dugout , locker rooms and the Green Bay Packers practice fields, getting a family picture with Coach Holmgren and sharing a private evening with the legendary Reggie White.

We also made it a point to catch professional sporting events around the country as we traveled to places like New York, Chicago, Minneapolis, Oakland and San Francisco. There were Big Ten Bowl games and witnessing the New York Marathon, standing at the finish line in Central Park. Besides the ten year anniversary trip to the Bahamas there were other family getaways to the Bahamas, Florida, California, Las Vegas and the Rocky Mountains including the spectacular Mount Rushmore, which involved a memorable RV trip. There was an annual New Year's Eve celebration that became a tradition where we would take over a suite at the Hyatt and enjoy time together as 5,000 balloons dropped into the atrium at midnight, and yes, it was another occasion for each one to bring a friend. But I always felt it was important to be together as a family as we closed out each year and opened a new one, always with a big breakfast and sometimes Mass at the church just a few blocks away.

Besides all the social opportunities it was a time to reflect on the accomplishments: the maturity and education gained, and the safety and health maintained over the years. They were all slowly moving along the path of life heading out on their own and not requiring my vigilant care like when they were younger. They could be self-sufficient if anything happened to me. It was a feeling of liberation after having had all the responsibility on my shoulders: day, month, year in and year out. Now they were growing to mature adults that could feed themselves, do their own laundry and be in charge of their own safety which included driving as they all had their licenses. Although I actually still made my youngest son's lunch through his junior year in high school, I was becoming a faucet that could be shut off in so many areas. Not to say that I stopped worrying ; that's something a parent never has the luxury of doing.

With that new feeling of freedom, I decided to take a friend up on an offer he made. He was overseeing radio properties in New Zealand and Australia. He offered to put me up and cover my expenses if I came Down Under to listen and offer some input on a couple formats that we had done so successfully in the states. In the past when I had offers like these or offers from friends to join them on an extended fishing trips, I always declined because I never felt I could indulge and be away for any extended time. There was also this determination to guard my safety so the kids would never be left orphaned. It kept me from doing certain things I would otherwise have loved to do, like the time I passed on an opportunity to get scuba diving certification in the Grand Caymans with a couple of business partners.

At a distance of over 10,000 miles away, my trip to New Zealand was not meant to be a long weekend, but rather an 8 day commitment. I asked my youngest son if he was interested in joining me, but he declined because he was committed to his cross country team that August in addition to the job he held. So off I went to the land Down Under of which I had heard so many positive things about, including the people, the scenery, the clean air and the technology they were known for.

Thanks to the international date line, I embarked and arrived on the same day. A journey from Wisconsin to Auckland, New Zealand took 17 hours in flight and an additional seven hours of layovers and customs through L.A.; in total a 24 hour trek. The country was everything I had heard and more. I met my friend and got busy listening to his station. After a few days we were in a public market called Victoria Station just walking, taking in the sights. I met a charming woman with the Kiwi accent indigenous to that country. We hit it off and talked for about a half hour. She was familiar with the local station I was there to help and my friend that brought me to New Zealand invited her to a party the station was hosting that night. I certainly had no intention of looking for someone to date that lived 10,000 miles away, but at the listener party later that evening we met again and there was a real attraction. She following me to America a couple weeks after I returned, and we started a relationship.

It had been a few years since my last separation and a couple years since the divorce was final, and I was open to finding a companion. And with the kids moving away it wouldn't be long before I was living alone with no one. And for the last 30 years I always had someone: beginning with Linda and if not a spouse then I had my kids with me. I wasn't sure how having a house to myself would be. But with the new feeling of liberation I had a desire to get involved with this unique individual from a different culture. At first we lived separately under one roof, then after a few months we made it official this was going to be a relationship with the intention of moving forward. It wasn't like me to live with someone without making a more serious commitment. But because of the extreme distance and the issue with visas and the limited opportunity that visa waivers offer, it was going to be a back and forth relationship as she would have to return to her homeland for extended periods of time to stay within the laws of immigration. After 9/11/01 it would become even more scrutinized.

Another realized obstacle to a long term relationship looking down the road was a consideration that because she had two adult children with forthcoming grandchildren quite likely, in fairness we would be living half the year in New Zealand, which in some respects certainly was attractive because of the country's beauty and simple lifestyle it would offer.

Like past relationships this one did not sit well with most of my children. But I wasn't too concerned because in the back of my mind the obstacle that 10,000 miles represented served as a built in restriction to keep me from moving too fast into marriage and making a mistake that was part of my history since Linda passed. And it was a good thing because this relationship faded amidst all the obstacles—almost as fast as it appeared. The cultural exchange and the worldly parts were very exciting, but a lifelong relationship didn't take hold and blossom.

This relationship started in the fall of 1999, and during this period (besides spending time trying to make the Pacific Ocean smaller while keeping focused on my job) there was a car accident involving my youngest son. It wouldn't come to settlement until four years later in 2003. At the time of the accident, my son was 2 months short of his 18th birthday which meant he was a minor and as he was the driver sited in the accident, I would be party to any lawsuit.

It started out as a celebration. Earlier in the day, my son's varsity cross country team won the Boys State Championship, a race both his older brothers and I attended. The girls from his high school had also won the Girls State Championship—an occasion for special celebration since its unusual for both the boys and girls teams to come out victorious. Later that night, which happened to be Halloween, the boys were at the home of one of the girl's who was hosting a get together. My son was driving the family Jeep Cherokee (I always liked having a sturdy car to hedge against any accidents.) He had four other team members in the car. One passenger rode in the front seat and the other three sat in the back seat. All were buckled in. There was no alcohol or drugs involved but there was speeding involved as an unknown car started to chase the vehicle my son was driving.

They weren't familiar with the car chasing them. They really didn't know why they were being pursued, so they were intent on eluding the chase vehicle. A game of cat and mouse ensued while turning down darkened streets in an attempt to elude the chasers. He ended up going 45 to 50 miles an hour down a private road that was intended for travel at 25 mph. The private development they turned into was relatively new and they had not yet posted a warning sign for an upcoming 90 degree turn. That is when he lost control of the vehicle and it crashed into a line of trees. After seeing the crashed vehicle, it's a wonder there were any survivors. Fortunately, the three boys in the back seat were unharmed. On the other hand, the front seat passenger had head trauma and a fractured neck requiring a Flight For Life lift to the emergency room. My son had not escaped injury either: he had a fractured neck.

When I received the call from one of the other fathers, my heart sank. I had let my guard down. It had been about 9 years since my oldest son first got his license and with the other two children driving many times in between and worrying a parent's worry every time they were driving. There had never been an accident and I was probably not worrying anywhere near as much as I did in the first years of each one driving and probably thinking I was going to escape any tragic driving accidents with my kids— and then I got the midnight call. The other father wasn't aware of the status of anyone, only that there had been a serious accident. I made the half hour drive to the hospital feeling completely numb not knowing if my son was alive—it was a serious accident.

I got to the hospital before the ambulance did. When it arrived minutes later it didn't have the siren or lights flashing. I immediately wondered what that implied. Did it mean there was no urgency because my son had perished? It was a parent's worst nightmare. As the paramedics pulled out the gurney I saw there was life. I thanked God and his mother, his guardian angel. The worst of my fears was unfulfilled. But he was seriously injured with a fracture of the cervical spine at the C7 vertebrae in his neck. After a stay at the first hospital he was taken to because of proximity, he was relocated to a medical college based hospital for more specialized treatment and released about a week later. They decided against a neck fusion procedure, instead opting to let the fracture heal itself. This required him to be immobile in a hospital bed that I ordered for his room so he could heal at home.

The thing about being the nice parent and allowing your son to drive others when they rely upon you for transportation, (and covering the expenses of the car, the gas and so forth) is that you are personally liable for any mishaps. You are the target. And it wasn't long before the parents of the passenger in the front seat filed a lawsuit against the driver, my son.

And because my son was just under legal age, I became the codefendant as the party being sued. With all the delays common to court systems and all the tactics lawyers are famous for including extensions, interrogatories, and depositions, the case dragged out for nearly four years. And it was four years of hell. First dealing with my son's recovery, followed by the uncertainty and anxiety surrounding his future health prospects, and finally the emotional and financial struggles brought on by the extended legal battle. One of the first things I had to see through were the charges being considered against him. They wanted to charge him with reckless endangerment. I met with the District Attorney overseeing the case and reasoned with him. As soon as the passenger's health status and future was determined, the D.A. was able to decide the charge against my son. The passenger ultimately recovered from his injuries. My son received a citation instead of the more indelible and serious charge. The thing I kept thinking was "Thank God he is alive! Thank God he is alive!" When he realized there was a 90 degree turn coming, his maneuvering prevented them from striking a huge oak tree straight on, which I believe would have meant certain death—perhaps for all of them.

My insurance company only paid the limits of the $125,000 coverage I carried. Over the years I had my checklist to keep everything straight, and when the annual casualty premiums were due I paid them and moved on to the next household need. I never considered an umbrella policy because I never had the luxury of taking the time to research deeper into insurance products. However, after my experience with that incident, I have recommended umbrella policies to all my friends as insurance well worth the cost in dealing with the unknowns of future tragedy.

When the insurance company fulfilled its responsibility I was on my own. In 2003, the plaintiff finally settled for $400,000. I was also responsible for my attorney's fees, totaling over six figures. And there was another cost: I swear I felt it took years off my life. But in the larger scheme of things, my son was alive, and that was all that mattered.

But that wasn't what was really really bad.

Chrysanthemum_hypargyrum

CHRYSANTHEMUM

Precious One

11

GETTING IT RIGHT

In 2003 I was finally able to cap the accident litigation geyser, stopping that particular flow of stress and upset in my life. It was also to be the year that my personal life would finally take a positive turn. By this time my oldest son and his wife had a 3 year old son. My second son had married his high school sweetheart the year before. My daughter was 23 and would marry in a couple of years having first met her husband to be at high school, and then again at the place they both worked. And my youngest son was into his third year of college. Each one was well onto their own road and establishing their own family history. And I was on my own now, too. Although I enjoyed my freedom and flexibility, I was still programmed to be with someone; yet I certainly wasn't going to force it, nor did I have to.

Earlier that year, some friends recommended that I call someone named Jodi, whose husband had passed away suddenly about a year earlier. Initially I resisted the idea, having acclimated to my new life over recent years. Then one day I decided to place the call. It was during the fall of 2003. Because my memory was long on the difficulties of bringing someone in to be part of my family, I was in no hurry to start down another path to potential disappointment. But that all changed from the first day I met Jodi. She was one of the most genuine individuals I had ever met .She was kind, thoughtful and beautiful.

After I introduced myself to her over the phone, she explained that she had not gone on a date in the 15 months since her husband passed away. She also spent the first five minutes on the phone telling me how she wasn't good at small talk. After chatting nonstop about 15 minutes, I pointed out that her small talk skills were much better than she'd given herself credit for. I asked her if she was a Bruce Springsteen fan and if she would be interested in seeing him in concert the next weekend. Understanding that she was just getting back into the dating scene after a long marriage, I suggested a get together at a sports bar midway between our respective residences where we could meet for a beverage and that if she was not comfortable with me I would give her the pair of concert tickets and she could go with whomever she chose. Our first get together—intended to be about an hour to just meet face to face—lasted over six hours. I presented her with a small gift that had a miniature box of Godiva chocolates on top. She pulled back the gift wrap to see a paperback version of the book The Art of Small Talk. It was my insurance plan in case we had an uncomfortable silence and it was to help her relax knowing we could always defer to the book. Of course, the book was never needed. Two days later we saw Springsteen together and we have been together ever since. We married about a year later and ten years later, I still find her to be the most amazing woman; I simply could not have picked anyone better as a partner. She has a special affinity for infants and toddlers and with her outgoing personality she is easily the favorite in any room. After so many false starts and wrong turns, I finally got it right.

Jodi had two daughters who, at the time we met, were in their early twenties and both in college. Given the maturity of all our children, we thought that we wouldn't face severe challenges in blending our families. With my past experiences etched so indelibly in my mind, you'd think I would have been more seasoned on the subject. But thinking that we could escape from family blending issues because none of our six kids would be living under the same roof with us was being naïve.

By late 2006, my oldest son and his wife had four children of their own. They were both receptive and welcoming to Jodi from day one. This was especially the case as three of their four children were born after Jodi was in my life, and have only known her as Grandma, a role that wonderfully suits her love of children. The grandkids treasure her as a gift and someone very special in their lives. The same can be said for their father. And our daughter-in-law enjoys a warm personal relationship with Jodi as a resource and package of love .

Recently, as a gift to me, my oldest son wrote a synopsis of his life growing up expressing appreciation for his upbringing and his feelings towards Jodi, which I will share in its entirety.

Dear Dad,

As part of Christmas this year, I wanted to give you something unique: an all encompassing thank you note. As a family, we have been through a lot together. Through it all, you have been a great example of leadership. Not once do I recall you complaining about our situation, or the fact that you were a single parent and had major responsibility with four kids to raise and a business to run. Not once did I see you quit. You always made things happen. You persevered through the toughest of tough situations in an unselfish manner. How you ran a household and a business is something I will never understand. While we were busy being kids, you were busy being two people.

The late eighties and early nineties provided many challenges. You worked hard to mask those challenges with fun, while providing the best education out there. Whether it was my time at St John Vianney or four great years at Catholic Memorial High School, the gift of Catholic education is something I will forever cherish. Who knew that CMH would connect me with my future wife in the spring of 1990? As my wife and I grow as parents, we see the full value of hard work and dedication to something we believe in. There is no doubt that private school tuition provides a challenge to the household, but when we both reflect on what our parents needed to sacrifice to make it happen, we take pause and move forward knowing that we are doing the right thing. With our Catholic upbringing comes another gift of spending Sundays together in church. It's a challenge to get four kids out the door every Sunday... yes, but you did it on your own. When we were on vacation we still went to church, we never missed a Sunday. You were consistent and disciplined. I can tell you one of my favorite things to do as a family is attend church weekly with my family. Thank you for the great education and most importantly, my faith.

On the social side of things, I have great memories of you taking us to NBA games on a regular basis. Front row to every game we went to. Spoiled is an understatement. It was not only a treat to sit just feet away from Larry Bird, Magic Johnson and Michael Jordan, it was a treat to remember doing it with my dad. Annual New Years at the Hyatt is another fond memory. Then there were the concerts! The Stones, Paul McCartney, Mellencamp, U2, The

Eagles, Tom Petty, Dave Matthews, and Jimmy Buffett—the list is almost endless! If there was a concert we wanted to go to, you provided the ticket. The memories of seeing some of the best artists on the planet were provided by you. If there was a trip to the Dells or skiing at Devil's Head, we were allowed to bring a friend. You never once said, "It is already hard enough going four on one." You gave us as much normalcy as possible. You also showed us first hand that taking on a little more in life is okay and that it is important to step out of our comfort zones. Thank you for always providing entertainment and most of all: fun.

The popcorn truck you introduced as a family bonding experience: naming it Linduas Liberator. Lindua, of course, was polish for Linda, something I remember grandma occasionally calling Mom. And then writing all of our names on the hood of the truck. The Liberator suggested that if we worked hard and made money it would provide us with liberation in the form of college education or maybe a car. But it was a business lesson that included pricing, inventory control, employee management, product offerings, audience enticements, mechanical engineering and licenses. Let's see ... pricing commercials, controlling sales and promotion inventory, employee management, choosing between Dr. Phil and Dr. Oz, an entire department of engineers and of course , an FCC license! There is a lot to be said about the parallels of running a popcorn truck and running the television station I am now in charge of overseeing. What a great opportunity! Your vision provided a path to future business success for me. Thank you!

You took time to go to all of our sporting events. I vividly recall you being at all my track and cross country meets. You didn't show-up to show-up, you were there with keen interest. You provided feedback at every one of my races: splits, strategic positives and negatives etcetera. Any parent can show-up and sit in the stands; you participated.

You were insistent that I not get a car right away, making me wait a little longer. I did not agree with that decision at the time, but I certainly understand it now. That decision was wise parenting and something I will never forget. Thank you for protecting me.

When it came time to move into our family home I remember you going over the plans carefully. Living on a lake was a new experience for all of us. The building of the retaining wall was a family event. It was hard work with a return we enjoy to this day. Driving up to the house is a treat. Remembering the pallets of stone and all the hard work that we put into that project. Not only were we building a wall, we were building a family memory. I remember you saying we could have paid a company to do all the landscaping, but why do that when we can do it ourselves and provide a sense of accomplishment at the same time.

When it came time for my fiancé and I to get married, you were very excited. You sat down with the entire family to go over the plan. I could tell just how much this meant to you. From helping with the band or the reception at the Club, everything was a blast. And including Mom in the ceremony was icing on the cake. It truly was a perfect day.

Then in June 2000 another chapter started with the arrival of our son. With him being the first grandchild, we thought it was only appropriate to include your name as part of his. From the start he had the benefit of having an incredible grandpa: donuts, motorized kid's vehicles, secret handshakes , T.G.I.F. and boating fun on the lake are just a few of the wonderful memories he already talks about. And then another brother and the twins came along, each with their own personality and interest. Each enjoys spending time with Grandpa—and why not?

When Jodi became part of our lives it was unbelievable. The nurturing that only a mother can provide was brought into our home. My wife had a true mother-in-law that has become a great friend. Our four children have an incredible grandmother that truly cares. Most importantly, you have an incredible partner. We could not be happier for you. Thank you for bringing Jodi into our lives.

You have taught us to respect others, put in more than you take out, and always put other people before ourselves. You have taught us that life is not fair, but it is important to push forward and be productive, not complacent. You have taught that faith is a powerful thing. Nobody or thing is more important than God. You have taught us to be humble and creative. You have taught us to be good parents and even better spouses.

Thank you for putting way more in than you have ever taken out. Thank you for all the gifts you have given me—most important being my education and my faith. I promise to pay it all forward as a gift to my children: the ultimate thank you to you.

I love you Dad. And I appreciate everything that you have done for me and my family.

Merry Christmas.

My oldest son and his family truly have an appreciation for his upbringing and respect and love for my wife. Maybe he got it because he was the oldest at twelve when his mother passed away, or maybe he understood it all because he has four of his own to put it in perspective. And at the time he wrote the letter his four were at the ages that basically matched the ages of my four when they lost their mother so he could clearly relate. Or maybe he is just different. As parents will mostly attest, each of their children are noticeably different from one another even though they breathe the same air, grow in the same environment, are similarly educated, and they share the same DNA, they manage to be unique.

By contrast, my other three children seldom shared the same appreciation despite being treated with the same opportunities and attention as I raised them. They never accepted Jodi's daughters and they minimally accepted Jodi. As in the past, there was a sense of proprietorship and unwillingness to accept someone new. Through the first five years of our marriage they never really embraced her, creating occasional awkward and defensive positions, which I have learned were part and parcel to blending families— even when not under the same roof— especially the families I tried to blend over the years.

My daughter was moving in the direction of greater acceptance after her first child was born in 2008. In fact, she would use Jodi to babysit her son while she went to work or ran errands, dropping him off to spend the day with her, calling her Grandma. I guess it can be said that when you trust your baby in someone's hands, you have confidence in the relationship.

This went on even after her son celebrated his first birthday. And why not as Jodi loves little babies.

Up to that point all were at least cordial; mostly distant to the relationship but everyone was essentially civil and when trying to move forward that was going to have to be good enough. I understand that they saw failed attempts I made as I spent the better part of the last two decades trying to become whole individually and as a family. But I suspect they never considered the part they played in adding to the difficulties or how challenging it was with the multiple personalities involved, with the proprietorship and protection that naturally exists on all sides when blending and getting over the loss of their mom, the many inherent challenges with the situation. As adult children they were just that, children without the ability to imagine or walk in my shoes. Their views were their views and because of simple ignorance to what it takes they were unwilling to open their minds to just maybe see it as their oldest brother and his family so clearly do.

By early 2009 a firestorm was brewing that was ignited by a simple and relatively benign event. And this wasn't even what was going to be really really bad!

Lactuca sativa

YELLOW CARNATION

Rejection

12

THE FIRESTORM

It was Christmas of 2007, and we were gathered in the great room of the home where Jodi and I lived. All four of my children were there: Dan, his wife and our four grandchildren, Michael and his wife, and Lynn and her husband, who were expecting their first child the next month. My youngest son, Joseph, was also there, accompanied by his wife to be. After opening and enjoying the gifts, we talked about the challenges of creatively selecting gifts for each other every year. Someone suggested that for the next Christmas, perhaps the gift of airfare could be given, allowing everyone to spend Christmas week together in sunny, warm Florida at a place we had recently established there. It would be similar to before they were married when we got together for our March getaways.

I thought it was a great idea: a wonderful way for the family to be together enjoying a desirable climate, rather than our cold, gray upper Midwest winters. And it would solve the challenges of deciding what to get everyone for Christmas. Past gifts had included things like yard heaters, fondue chocolate makers and other gadgets and items that combined elements of fun and practicality. This new plan would really simplify the process.

Having planned many family trips in the past, I knew that logistics could be a nightmare. Considering the individual complexities of work schedules for each of my children and their spouses, I elected to present everyone their 2008 Christmas gift via a check in February, allowing them to book their own tickets. The plan was to overlap our visits for at least a few days with Christmas day being the center of everyone's holiday schedule.

When Christmas arrived, only Dan and his family made it to our Florida holiday. My other two sons (or their partners) had job conflicts during Christmas week, which was unfortunate considering that most work activity is reduced during those days between Christmas and New Year. They all arrived the following week after we had already returned to our own jobs and responsibilities back home. Lynn, her husband and their one year old son also had to cancel because of a sick dog they could not abandon. They were really looking forward to this trip. We promptly scheduled another trip to Florida for their family for March in which we would join them—by then their dog was back to health and able to be left with a kennel.

Our make up trip in March of 2009 was a nice time spent with Lynn's family. Their little boy was 14 months and relished the attention of Grandpa and especially Grandma, who has a special affinity for little people. We made a point to allow my daughter and her husband some "date time," encouraging them to take our car and get away. We arranged an evening out giving them a gift card for dinner and some vouchers for entertainment. We also made a couple trips to the beach, took many pictures, measured our grandson on the growth chart measuring board for future posterity, and spent quality pool time taking advantage of the glorious weather.

There was a scare the night they went on one of their dates. Their son had been running a fever from a cold. He was receiving Children's Tylenol every 4 hours. At the end of our babysitting night right before his parents came home we gave him another dose of his medication. It was shortly thereafter that he experienced a fibril seizure. He became listless and non-responsive and it scared the hell out of us. We called 911 and summoned emergency medical help. It seemed like an eternity, but they finally arrived and took him to the local hospital. My daughter rode along inside the emergency vehicle with her son, while our son-in-law, my wife and I followed in a car behind, all the while freaked out about what was happening. As it turned out, we didn't need to wait the prescribed four hours for the next dose of Tylenol to break his fever. Instead, they recommended administering Children's Ibuprofen within two hours during periods of high fever. The spike in this temperature and his listlessness were the result of the medication transition reaction.

The experience brought back nightmare memories for Jodi, who seven years earlier had made a 911 call when her husband never woke from his sleep. He died from a massive heart attack at the very young age of 54.

Jodi frequently helped my daughter out by babysitting so she could go to work, run errands and take care of things more freely. Fortunately, my wife was retired and had been available over the last five or more years to do something she really enjoyed: taking care of the grandkids including my oldest son's four and now Lynn's child.

Earlier Lynn had approached me about the possibility of cleaning our house in order to earn extra cash. Since we already had someone coming every other week I thought it would be a good way to keep the money in the family, so I asked my wife and she agreed that it made sense. One day as Lynn was cleaning, she came across something in one of the guest bedrooms in a closet dresser inside one of the drawers. It was a homemade bong made from a punctured hole in a miniature apricot juice can. She had found it in an earlier cleaning before actually making me aware of it. As the last person to use that room was Jodi's youngest daughter, (who was 24 at the time) it was assumed that it belonged to her. I have no experience with items like bongs since I never smoked weed, but Lynn was certain that was what the little can had been used for.

Lynn ignored it at first, but later decided that I needed to know since this was the house I lived in, and if something illegal was going on, I should be made aware of it. My response probably wasn't as heated as she was expecting. Over the years of raising my kids we never had any drug or alcohol issues, in part due to my example of not partaking in either, and as a general policy—it was never an issue. But at this stage I was not raising this individual who was an adult and whose frequency in the house at that time was maybe once or twice a year because she lived on the west coast. So I didn't get upset or feel a need to counsel; I didn't think that this was going to be a recurring issue. I did ask to see the item so I could be educated, and I assured Lynn that I planned to mention it to Jodi, thinking that she would want to address the issue with her daughter. And of course, she did: telling her daughter that it was irresponsible and unacceptable. Her daughter apologized for her actions and promised never to do it again. I really did not think it was a big deal, or anything I needed to be overly concerned about. But I was wrong.

After I mentioned the issue to my wife I found out that she was offended that Lynn did not come directly to her with this finding, but chose to reveal the matter to me instead. Jodi and I had been married and living in this house for five years—effectively sharing it equally. When we married we had the house appraised and included it as part of our prenuptial agreement. Jodi actually contributed half of the equity of the property value, so in every sense this was her place equally, not just mine, and the children were all made aware of her investment above and beyond the marriage.

But I'm sure my daughter, programmed from years earlier, still looked at this as my place, so she came to me. But Jodi felt hurt and betrayed by the fact that Lynn hadn't come directly to her in a matter that involved her daughter. She had been working hard to develop a solid relationship with Lynn, which was not an easy thing to do considering all the maternal example disappointments that riddled my daughter's journey to adulthood and the emotional wall of protection she'd built along the way. Still, Lynn had come to rely on Jodi, even entrusting her young son into Jodi's care, so it could be assumed that a significant level of confidence in the relationship existed. Up to that point, things between them had definitely been moving in the right direction. They had bonded somewhat over the mutual love and care of Lynn's child, and that was galvanized even further that terrible night in a Florida emergency room. In addition, Jodi had been attentive in so many other ways over the previous five years: making meals and dropping them off at Lynn's house, providing discount coupons on items Lynn liked and occasionally slipping in a one hundred dollar bill when financial challenges were clear. She took Lynn maternity clothes shopping and sat at the hospital with her while she was receiving an IV drip for dehydration while her husband needed to be at work. She let Lynn borrow her car and made herself available to watch the baby and help out whenever possible. In short, Jodi put a lot of time and care into building a loving relationship with Lynn, and she felt that they were close enough that the bong issue should have been a matter for direct conversation between them.

Instead, Jodi felt Lynn's choice to address the matter to me was Lynn's way of tattling on Jodi's daughter. There had never been any real acceptance of Jodi's daughters on Lynn's part, just as there were always challenges whenever I attempted to blend my family over the years. Jodi felt that Lynn's action showed disregard for her feelings, the care and efforts she'd made, her place as an equal share owner of the home, and her role as the mother of the person being accused.

After explaining her feelings and the resulting shouting match on the phone between them, my wife suggested that they just agree to disagree and move on. They weren't seeing eye to eye on this, which can happen in life, but they shouldn't throw everything away over such a benign incident.

I figured that a lot of what my daughter was experiencing was from the past and had little to do with Jodi, who had only been a positive force in her life. I realized that my daughter was really slanted on this when she left me a voicemail saying, "Dad, I expect you to pick Jodi over me." My response was, "There is no picking one over the other. You are my daughter and Jodi is my wife. I love you both."

Once again I found myself in the middle—an all too familiar and unenviable place to be.

Webster's New World dictionary defines the word firestorm as an intense fire over a wide area, such as one caused by an atomic bomb explosion with its high winds. This situation was building to be one horrible, nightmare of a firestorm. The flames were being fanned by ghosts of the past and it was about to spread to a wide area within my family. No matter how much I pleaded with my daughter not to confuse anything or anyone from the past with the reality of what existed currently, and to just move on and put it behind us, she wouldn't listen.

Instead, she incited her younger brother to anger, and he didn't need much encouragement. Our version of the atomic bomb became known as the "atomic bong" incident. It was not only a catalyst, but it became the excuse to vent on everything they understood and didn't understand from their mother's illness onward. The facts didn't necessarily matter. In a burning flashover, Joseph directed a fiery, ranting, raving email at me and my wife in connection with the bong incident—a situation he had nothing to do with nor did he fully understand. His message was several pages long and heavily peppered with profanity. It slammed Jodi for being a horrible mother to her kids and berated me for being a horrible father for not defending and taking his sister's side. It was full of venom, foul language, and anger at our father-son history. Much of it was in upper case, as if he was yelling the whole time. He also declared that we would not be invited to his upcoming wedding planned for the following year. We were to have nothing to do with his wedding plans, rehearsal , or ceremony and we would certainly not be welcome in any wedding day pictures. I did not exist to him.

This terrible declaration wasn't softened by time over the next year—not in the slightest. We did attend the ceremony because as he said the bride's parents requested that we be there, but he made sure that we were not included on any invitation or website, that we were not welcome the night before at the family rehearsal, and that we did not appear in any wedding day photos. It was painful, stressful and monumentally sad. None of this can ever be made good.

In retrospect, I guess that I saw it coming, but I could never have imagined the severity. The year before on my birthday I arranged for Dan, one of his sons, my wife, Joseph and his then fiancé to have a nice dinner together and attend an NBA basketball game. Our sets of seats were in different parts of the arena, but the intention was to switch at halftime so that everyone could sample at least part of the game in the premium seats. It was an arrangement we had made during previous games and was designed to be fair for everyone. Joseph and his fiancé sat in the preferred seats for the first part of the game, and I was to take my grandson over after halftime and give Joseph my tickets to sit in the seats we just vacated. But something happened where he left before we got to the premium location, so I was unable to give him our tickets for the second half. And he was unable to get back into the premium area to retrieve the other tickets. Come to find out, he was convinced that we were purposely ditching him. He called my cell phone a number of times, but that concrete facility is notorious for bad or dropped signals, so I never heard his call attempts or got a voicemail message. Still, he was absolutely convinced that I had ditched him. My response was to ask him when had I ever ditched him before? Why would I ditch him? I spent years organizing special family time and events for the purpose of being together. There was no history or reason to ditch him and his date. Yet afterwards he was so adamant that he was right that while having this discussion he threw me out of his condo because I wouldn't admit to what he was convinced of in his head—a total misconception fueled by his deep rooted anger. The facts and the truth were not consistent with the anger he held inside, but he could not see it for himself.

Here was my youngest son, a person that I had loved and cared for from the moment of his birth. I helped feed, clean and rock him. As he grew, I carried him many times as a toddler because he had casts on both feet to stretch his heel cords so he could walk someday. I played with him and shared lots of time together with his mom through his first five years in various activities. And then, of course, just as he turned five, he was solely my responsibility when his mom passed. In truth, he was solely mine at four while his mom battled cancer and chemotherapy. His care was all mine: his safety, his education, his social development, his nutrition and entertainment. All the known and unknown was my responsibility. All the financial resources required to raise a child were my responsibility. Caring for accidents was also my responsibility, whether it was running into a fireplace hearth requiring stitches, sled riding into a neighbor's fence requiring stitches, or a serious car accident requiring bedside care while he recovered from a broken neck and paying lawyers to defend and settle the resulting lawsuit with plaintiffs.

My support took the form of countless registrations, reservations and sports practices, matches, games and races. When it was time for college, I covered his tuition and living expenses for six years. There were the moves to and within his college community, the assisted move back from Denver on a Thanksgiving weekend—things any dad would be happy to provide. To celebrate his graduation I presented him with a new car. Afterwards I made a significant financial gift that allowed him to complete a down payment on a condo and have money left over to make improvements..

After all the love and emotional and financial support I'd showed him over the years, he only had deep anger for me and he expressed it for everyone connected to us to see on his wedding day. I tried for months before the wedding to reach out to him and somehow reconcile, but he never answered or returned my calls, going so far at one point to change his number. So when the day of the ceremony arrived, we attended, but being unwelcomed in every way we chose to sit near the back of the congregation in an effort to avoid any unpleasant scenes or be accused of disrupting their special day.

Unlike Joseph, Lynn did eventually allow some communication with me. But any suggestion on my part to encourage even a minimal relationship with my wife was stonewalled. She would not have anything to do with her, despite being reminded of how difficult it was making it for everyone involved to just have any sense of civil family life.

In looking back, I believe that this was the first time they saw real commitment from a spouse of mine. Jodi was undeniably kind, thoughtful and genuine. Our marriage was into its fifth year and doing great, and it was clear that Jodi wasn't going to leave on her own or be eased out by anyone. My past relationships had always been impacted by my kids' unwelcoming attitudes and emotional resistance, contributing in part to their stresses and eventual downfall.

But Jodi was different and things in my children's lives were different. Three of them were now married with the fourth soon to be married; everyone had partners and lives of their own. Yet there was still obvious resentment by some when such deep anger bubbled to the surface over a seemingly trivial incident.

I'm convinced that Michael, Lynn and Joseph weren't consciously aware they had been waiting for something to spark their deeply repressed feelings to ignite an emotional firestorm. Still, the displays of disrespect, loose profanity, arrogance and general disregard for the efforts of others on their behalf were extremely hurtful and resulted in extended periods of estrangement. I think the dichotomy was that part of each of them really wanted me to ultimately have a partner in life, just as their mom suggested in the love tape she left for me. She wanted me to have a full life and to be happy. After all, they each had their spouses and were starting their families. But I believe another deeper part of them resented the idea of me finding happiness with someone other than their mother. The 5, 6 and 9 year olds inside of them that witnessed their mother's passing was emotionally stunted, unable in some ways to grow past the hurt. In their eyes, no one could ever be allowed in their mother's place and somehow lessen or usurp their glowing, loving memory of her—especially not someone with children of her own.

Linda's passing instantly forged my soul with more compassion; I found shortly afterwards that I couldn't keep from crying at a movie with even a mildly sentimental plot, and it changed how I viewed and responded to others and their struggles. In contrast, I believe Linda's passing subtly ingrained a sense of anger in some of my children, clouding out the compassion in their hearts since they felt they had received none in having their mother stolen by disease and death when they were so young and vulnerable.

But that wasn't what was really really bad.

Tagetes erecta

MARIGOLD

Grief and Pain

13

WHAT WAS REALLY REALLY BAD

A shocking and unexpected cancer diagnosis was followed by months and months of dreadful chemotherapy. The death of the love of my life and partner of 20 years and then having to share that tragedy with our four young children. A funeral week that was surreal. A slew of housekeeper disappointments and nanny nightmares that acted as speed bumps and potholes to disrupt our path to a smooth transition. A painful divorce followed by a new marriage in an effort to serve all the family needs only to be followed by another life disrupting, distracting divorce. A near fatal accident that involved flight for life followed by a bed-bound recovery and four years of lawsuit proceedings resulting in heavy financial and emotional costs. Attempting the difficult, delicate balancing act of blending families. Dealing with the frustration and heartbreak of grievously disrespectful adult children. Weathering the pain and confusion of estrangement from those children. Having my phone calls blocked. Having my emails rejected and letters returned to sender. Gifts sent for grandkids were returned to sender. Closing out a thirty year career with a retirement party attended by some 300 friends, employees and members of the community with three children noticeably absent. Dealing with a constant stream of jealousy, immaturity, ignorance, arrogance and anger over imagined wrongs. Being shut out and ignored on my own son's wedding day. All of this was certainly really bad.

It's amazing how when I catalog all the challenges and distractions into one paragraph how it is done rather quickly. But when I break down each episode into the stress, turmoil and suffering it represented, it makes me wonder how I'm still standing. But as time unfolds and one more chapter in life is revealed I've realized that things weren't truly bad in comparison to the isolation, helplessness and hopelessness that followed. What was really really bad was that after all the investment of time, attention and unconditional love in raising children and looking forward to an adult relationship with them, they have become estranged from me instead. These children had reached a stage in their mid twenties and thirties when appreciation, pragmatic thought, compassion and the ability to forgive and put things in proper perspective normally takes hold in an adult personality. Instead they each regressed in thoughts and actions back to the time of their childhood and its tragedy, completely disregarding the subsequent care, attention and support they received, instead lost in their pathological grief, unable to recognize logic ,love and family.

For the last few years all three children have rejected any opportunity for communication and reconciliation. The absolute worst part is that I have many of the answers as to why they have withdrawn (although not all the answers because until they open up and talk, we will never uncover the deeper reasons). And through seeking professional feedback I have significant understanding of some of the issues they face and the assistance they can get to help them understand and work through their issues. But they won't communicate with me; which makes me feel incredibly frustrated and helpless.

My children have intentionally changed phone numbers, home addresses and email contact information with a firm unwillingness to share any contact information. They've exhibited the same treatment to many aunts and uncles, and even their own in-laws who have reached out with notes or simple seasonal greetings—all returned or ignored. The hardest aspect to accept is their refusal to consider any kind of professional help or mediation. Many times over the years I have offered to join them in sessions even though two of the three live out of state. No matter the distance, I would make it happen. And if their insurance was an issue, I have been clear that I would pay any out of pocket expenses so there would be no financial burden to them. But they do not respond.

In the past when they would respond, it was with arrogance: they already had all the answers and psychological counseling or family mediation wouldn't change the past—insisting it would be a good idea for me, but it wasn't necessary for them. It is a mentality and unwillingness to open their minds and hearts to the possibility of displaced anger and their own pathological grief that stems back to the loss of their mother and the resulting abandonment issues. But there is no way they could ever cast any negativity towards their mother and her sacred, protected memory, and understandably so. Except they don't fully understand how that dynamic gets in the way of reality.

Over the past twenty years I have sought consistent professional guidance from an experienced family therapist; you don't survive all I have been through on your own without some guidance. The frustration I feel as a parent is finally coming to understand the buried issues yet being faced with their refusal to avail themselves of the help to understand and diffuse those issues. It's like seeing your child with a drug , alcohol or food addiction. You reach out to help them but they block your efforts or they insist that you are the one with the problem. It's a feeling of total helplessness. Other than the generic statement, "You made your choices," it has not been clear what exactly it is that has stirred this separation and hate because they won't reveal it.

As the therapists say, if they were to ever stop blaming me, they would then have to address their anger, and whatever that anger is, they currently don't have the understanding or courage to face it. Therefore, it is much easier to pin that anger on me and then bury their heads in the sand, refusing to explore things any further.

The helplessness I have experienced as a parent feels insurmountable. As parents we are wired to assist and protect. One of the cornerstones of the responsibility is to use our years of experience and wisdom to help our children avoid situations that will leave them with regrets. We never want to see our children hurt or sad. We want them to avoid bad choices and the consequences of those bad choices. Parents suffer right along with their children in bad times. Knowing we can't live their lives, we accept that we must release them to grow on their own and that everyone (even our children) must learn from their mistakes so that they can gain wisdom from their own unique experiences.

Along the way, three of my adult children have formed an alliance against me which falsely empowers them. Because they feel the comfort of consensus, they don't consider that they could all be suffering from the same emotional problems. History has shown time and again that consensus alone isn't proof that a belief or course of action is correct. Still, my children huddle together in their mutual conflict with me because it is the easiest path, whereas examining the root causes of their feelings and subsequent actions might lead to the discovery of errors and misconceptions on their part—a prospect that is too costly and difficult to face. Would a little humility and openness be too much to pay in exchange for peace of mind and family happiness for each of our generations to share?

As I've always told them, "Doing the right thing is not always the easy thing." Additionally, if they ever had the awakening that the estrangement that has developed over the last few years was so very wrong, then they would have to acknowledge all their actions that can never be made good. These involve missed weddings, pregnancies, births and the precious infant and toddler years of grandchildren. All those opportunities to build loving memories were stubbornly thrown away with hurtful words and deeds based on deep seeded anger that was mostly misplaced. And if not that, then what? Certainly their anger and the resulting actions were not commensurate with the years of attention, love and opportunities they were afforded.

Michael had always been the most private of the four siblings. During his elementary and secondary school years he often kept to himself in his room doing homework with the door closed. He was a good student. He gave no cause for concern other than his affiliation with a friend of sometimes questionable character from across the street. When he was about ten years old, this friend pulled his pants down while my daughter was present and exposed himself. In junior high this same friend would join us occasionally for family outings, one of which was the annual New Year's Eve event at the Hyatt. On two successive years he drank illegally to the point of intoxication. I tried to explain to my son about my liability as the adult in charge should his friend get hurt or injure someone else. In his later teen years this same young man would eventually crash his car while driving intoxicated, killing himself and one other, and seriously injuring another passenger who lost a leg and almost his life. The surviving passenger was my son's roommate in college at the time. My son was upset with me because he felt that I didn't pay his friends' passing enough homage. He never considered, however, that my discouragement over the years of his spending time with this alcoholic friend may have kept him out of the car that fateful night.

Even into his adult years, my son always thought I was being unreasonable in discouraging involvement with this friend. I don't believe he ever truly understood the poor influence or danger in hanging around with this friend. Now that he has a son and daughter of his own he'll get some perspective on it as they grow older and he faces a similar experience, but this time in the role of the parent.

Michael said a number of revealing things to me in his early thirties before he had children. One thing I learned was that he was upset with me for not quitting my job when his mother was sick. He said that if his wife was sick (they did not have children at this time)as Mom was, that he would quit his job to be with her. I explained that I had financial responsibility for my wife and four children, and that my job provided the medical benefits to cover the treatment expenses and paid for our mortgage, tuition, groceries and other living expenses.

Since I didn't know whether my wife would survive two months or two years, it simply wasn't practical for me to leave my job. How would the bills get paid? And actually, as president of the company, I enjoyed significant flexibility to be available for all the treatments and general care during my wife's illness. I was available much more than I'm sure he realized. Most adults understand what is practical, but unfortunately not my 31 year old son. In his state of arrested development he was emotionally stuck as the 9 year old he was when his mother battled cancer.

I also learned that he had an unfortunate memory of a time that he had to help his mother to the bathroom. I'm sure it impacted him significantly and originated his thought that Dad should have been there. There were times after Linda passed that I know he felt I needed to be present during the day, rather than at work, when he was in scuffles with his older brother. Brothers sometimes don't get along, and the younger child usually gets the raw end of the deal in those situations. Michael blames me for not being present at those times—he can't be mad at Mom.

Once he asked me "How do you know that Mom and you would even be together after all these years?" I could only offer my optimistic take on the possibilities, but with his mother unavailable, all that was left was her voice on the taped message speaking about our very special love and relationship. But he wouldn't accept that testimony. Instead, chose to embrace a scenario that supports his anger and functions as an outlet for his emotional pain. He contended that with the divorce rate at one in two, Mom and Dad probably wouldn't have made it anyway. He supports this in his head with the memory of an argument or two we had to validate his conclusions. What he doesn't realize, though, is that most likely those arguments involved disciplining our children, a much debated subject between parents who each bring their own set of values, experiences and approaches to child rearing.

It seems to me that Michael has twisted things to support his anger. An example would be his disappointment over my wife and I not being able to attend a surprise thirtieth birthday party for him, held several months after his actual birthday. That particular weekend we already had airfares booked for a trip to celebrate our wedding anniversary. The trip also included ties to a work project. Instead, on his actual birthday, my wife and I made a ten hour round trip to bring him a gourmet meal that we prepared and we enjoyed a quality time focused on him and his actual special day. But that wasn't good enough. Our missing his big birthday party supported his anger.

On the day his son was born we went to the hospital to see and hold the baby. Earlier in the year Michael announced that we were never welcome to visit them at their home. Before the baby was born he also strongly discouraged, as he put it, "gifts, pre-gifts or pre-pre-gifts," or our showing any interest in the pregnancy— basically telling us to mind our own business. I thought grandchildren were our business. Despite numerous requests to visit them and our grandson after he was born, we were either declined or simply ignored. Then the ultimate scheme to hurt us was accomplished when our daughter-in-law became pregnant again and delivered a baby girl, all without our knowledge. We didn't find out until a birth announcement arrived in the mail 18 days after the fact. What was really really bad was that they denied us not only the anticipation during the pregnancy journey and the joy and excitement of the birth, but chance to be a part of something even more special than usual. This baby girl's birth date was the same as Michael's mother, and to commemorate that fact and honor Linda's memory they gave the child a derivative of her first name and the same middle name as her biological grandmother.

Carefully excluding me from the joy of such a blessed event, but making certain to mail me a confirmation of the occasion after the fact hit a new low of disrespect and outright cruelty. It was a burning arrow straight through the heart. How deep his anger must be! Although he insists that he is not angry, I have to wonder what emotion would drive a person to do these things?

A few months prior to shielding the second pregnancy and birth from us Michael went on a rage and demanded that I get professional help by seeing a specialist three times a week for six weeks. After that happened he would speak to the professional therapist himself to make sure they had all the details and then he might possibly allow communication with him and his family. The professional therapist found this demand to be most arrogant, as of course did I. But I was familiar with my son's arrogance. The amazing thing is that he was unaware that I had a 15 year relationship with an excellent family therapist with 40 years of experience in his field of family therapy. This professional knew our complete history and had actually met with a number of the principals in my life over the last 20 years.

I let Michael know that the therapist was willing to meet with him, listen and share the history along with his opinion. Initially, he accepted the offer to meet, but he ultimately canceled the day before, supposedly because I asked to sit in and observe. But I think it was a bluff on his part. I don't believe he ever intended to keep the appointment since he refused to return the therapist's follow up calls. It was a terrible disappointment. This was the closest he'd ever come to receiving help from a professional, but in the end he couldn't ... wouldn't go through with it.

Michael received daily care and support in the areas of education, nutrition, health, safety, social opportunities, entertainment and was even provided for in non-essential areas like braces, Lasik surgery, cosmetic surgery to fix a bump on his nose (under the guise of a deviated septum procedure) as well as a procedure for a heart oblation that was not life threatening but allowed him to be active in sports which he so enjoyed. Still, with all that I provided and saw to on his behalf, he somehow retained a resentful attitude toward me while growing up, feeling neglected or ignored and not feeling enough love. From his ninth year on he resented the absence of a mother's love in his life. I could provide for and satisfy the mother's checklist, but I couldn't fulfill the mother's love capacity.

Lynn stopped visiting using the argument with my wife as her excuse, completely cutting my wife off at that point. While she was still open to me for the first six months, she was clearly miffed that I was not completely in her camp and that I didn't back her side of the issue. About this time she and her family moved out of state, nearly a thousand miles away. It turns out that they also had some differences with her husband's siblings and in-laws and were also in the process of estranging themselves from that side of their family. The primary estrangement was from her mother-in-law due to personality conflicts, but she also had no plans to remain in touch with her father-in-law as he was in the mid stages of Alzheimer's disease. She said they wanted to remember him as he used to be, and not in the state he'd become. Truthfully, that was one of the most disheartening things a parent can hear coming out of the mouth of one of their children because it demonstrates a complete absence of compassion, especially for those left to do the care giving. Thank goodness the man's wife didn't feel that way, because otherwise, who would be there to love and care for him? It immediately brought to mind the movie The Notebook, which deals with this dreadful disease. For anyone familiar with Alzheimer's, there are many reasons why this movie pulls at your heart.

Lynn also became pregnant shortly afterwards. Once again, I was made aware of this not through happy news from my daughter herself, but from relatives who received the announcement via general mail. Yes, I was hurt by this as my daughter clearly didn't see the importance of sharing the news with me personally. In fact, she too blocked my calls and any communication from me during her pregnancy. She allowed me to visit about a month after the baby was born. During that visit I made a point of assuring them that I would happily fly back out for the baby's baptism. The baptism was held a couple of months after my visit, but they did not share the date with me. I found out about it several weeks after the event and again felt hurt that they didn't include me. It was my grandson's baptism! Up until that point I had been present at the baptisms of all five of my grandchildren. Lynn knew it was important to me but excluded me anyway.

Shortly after that I made my opinion known that I thought their decision to cut off her mother-in-law and ignore her father-in-law during his illness was an insensitive, poor choice. After that she blocked all communication from me: any gifts for the grandchildren or mail to them was returned to sender. This went on for over six months until I finally decided to make the thousand mile trip to their house to see them. When I got there she refused to answer the door. Instead, she sent me a text informing me that she had notified the police, explaining that I was unwelcome and to watch out for me.

I couldn't believe my eyes! She had called the police on me! I was dumfounded. Eventually, though, they allowed me to stop over the next night, but only after the kids were in bed. That hour or so exchange accomplished nothing. They still had frozen hearts and regarded my wife as someone unworthy of their acceptance. It wasn't just me being rejected as they proclaimed they had never been happier than the last year and a half since they moved away from home, leaving behind and shutting out communications with aunts, uncles, in-laws, and close friends from secondary school and college. Their statement was that "none of these people served them anymore" and they wanted to teach their children to "be mindful."

I asked how they would explain it when their kids got into school and they have grandparent's day or other kids talk about their grandparents, since they have made the choice to exclude grandparents on both sides. They had no answer for that. Clearly they were on the run from accountability. When people who love and know you expect valid, justifiable reasons for your words and deeds, the only choice is to run when you cannot provide them. I only hope they don't eventually run from their own children, who will also expect answers someday.

Because Joseph was the youngest of the four, there was no one beneath him requiring my attention, so he got all that was left over—perhaps too much as he was provided for in every possible way. It was all in my attempt to make up for the monumental loss that he and his siblings experienced.

There was some pulling away once Joseph went to college, but I felt that it was normal as kids spread their wings when they get into the undergrad rhythm of life. They try to extend this wing spreading at home when they return for the holidays and summer break. Most college parents have their own transition stories when their kids think they can walk in the door at three in the morning at home because that is their new found college rhythm. While Joseph was in college I approached him a number of times about the frequency of his hosting parties at the campus house he shared with some friends and his regular treks to the bars during the week. I was assured that everything was under control. But because of the university system's privacy measures I was unable to verify Joseph's GPA to compare his definition of "under control" with my own.

What a system! You fund the room and board, books and tuition, but the school won't share academic performance with you. (Try that business strategy with any other institution and see how many investors you can attract.) My son accused me of only caring because I paid the bills. And while I required some accountability from him while investing in his education, that was certainly not the only reason I was concerned. I cared about his performance just as I cared about him and his growth his entire life. It's a father's responsibility to pay attention and care. If I didn't, I'd be accused of being an apathetic parent.

As it turned out, Joseph took almost six years to get his undergraduate degree in Medical Microbiology and Immunology, finally graduating in 2006. In fairness, his subject matter was challenging, but his wavering discipline and focus made it even more challenging. After graduation, he had a short stint in Colorado. But while he was out there he realized that his future was back home. In college he had become reacquainted with a young woman he'd known since he was five. Their friendship had blossomed in love, and the gravity of his future was pulling him back east. It was Thanksgiving weekend in 2007 that I helped him pack a U-Haul and drive home. After living together in her parents' house for a year they began to search for a place of their own. My wife had a background as a real estate agent and helped them through the process. I provided a monetary sum as an early wedding gift that allowed them to contribute to a down payment along with some improvements and still have cash remaining from the gift.

Sadly, just after they moved into their new place our estrangement took root. It was as if he got a superb education funded, a new car as a graduation gift and the seed money to own and start building equity rather than renting as he and his wife to be were getting settled, and then he was done with me. Up until then I was only tolerated. It was within the next year and a half that my daughter had the dispute with my wife and Joseph used that as a launching point to pronounce that we were not to be a part of or have anything to do with his wedding: another promise painfully fulfilled. For the better part of the next four years he would not return my calls or respond to any of my emails. Many postal attempts were also ignored. The same went for attempts to communicate with his wife.

After about three years I received an email from Joseph— because he needed something that related to DNA and gene therapy. It was very important to him and his wife. His lengthy correspondence to me began with, "I know you still care, Dad, because you send notes and cards and wish me happy birthday, so

I'm hoping you will help me out here." I responded with a parent's unconditional love. In spite of all his intentional efforts to be hurtful and cruel over the last several years, I quickly provided him with the necessary information or sent it directly to the assigned laboratories as requested. As soon as it was received, they again would not respond to any email or phone call. In fact, both email address and cell phone numbers were changed not long after they got what they wanted from me.

I stopped by and knocked on the door when I saw a light on, only to get no answer and see the light turned off as I left. Then about a year later I figured I had nothing to lose, hoping that his heart had softened over time and that maybe he might be open to moving forward. So I waited for him to return home from work one day about 3:30 in the afternoon. I stood outside his garage where I could connect with him, giving him a hug and asking him for the opportunity to just talk. I had a loving message I wanted to share with him, so I typed it up in case I missed him. The message went as follows:

I hope I am able to see you in person to share these thoughts. Otherwise, I will leave them in your door.

First, this week makes it an incredibly lonely four years that you wrote me the email saying you wanted nothing to do with me. As I hope every day is the day that is reversed, I hope the same for today. I know that you have been very upset with me and that you have your reasons. Please know that I never in all the years meant to hurt you in any way. My intentions were always love, but I am not perfect. You will see in raising your son there are no perfect dads … just ones doing the best they know how.

I would hope that sometime soon you will remember ALL the good that I know outweighs the not so good. ALL the caring for and attention since you were an infant, and of course, all the details that had to be covered after mom passed.

Joseph, I have so many good memories that I could not even name them all, and all the day to day welfare that a dad is responsible for—much of which you started to learn a few months ago when your son was born. The point is there was so much good in a very challenging situation. I ask you to please find it in your heart to also remember some of that to help mitigate that which wasn't always right, and for which I apologize sincerely.

I can't put into words how much I miss you. Please let me show you.

Love Dad

My good intentions were met with rage when he arrived home, rushing his car into the garage. As I approached him he charged at me using profanity and demanding that I get off his property. I briefly tried to calm him, but there was no dowsing his anger. It was as if the fury-filled sentiments from that terrible email four years earlier still burned with the same intensity. The exchange lasted a few minutes at most and ended with one last bull rush towards me that pushed me with enough force to rip my watch off and leave a four inch cut on my wrist. At that point I simply stood back while the garage door closed and I pleaded with him to please just talk with me.

I mentioned him as the father of a son. They too conceived and never announced the pregnancy. The baby was born and they did not share news of his birth. I found out about it by accident as one of the well wishers from my daughter-in-law's work had errantly sent a congratulations card to my address, with just my last name and address. I forwarded the card so it could be received by my son and his wife. As any parent or grandparent can imagine, it is extremely hurtful when your kids use the withholding of a pregnancy and birth as a weapon against you. Especially when they live nearby—that's what is really really bad. And, once again, when it came time to baptize the baby, we were not informed or welcomed.

During the last few years those three adult children have found many new ways to be cruel and hurtful. It wasn't enough for them to totally ignore me with even a simple card acknowledging Father's Day over the last five years. (When they were young they occasionally presented me with Mother's Day cards in May in addition to Father's Day cards in June.) They also stopped even acknowledging my birthday. The feedback I would get was that they all felt really proud of this non-action. It didn't matter that I continued doing what I had had always done: call them at the exact time they were brought into this world on the date they were born. Fortunately for all, they were born at reasonable times: 7:53 a.m., 10:06 a.m., 11:35 a.m. and 12:01 p.m. This was just one of the rituals I felt was important to keep and never forget—kind of like playing Santa Claus for them every Christmas Eve until the youngest one outgrew the tradition.

After about two years, the compounded estrangement finally took its toll. The exceptional cruelty of Michael's actions to hide the pregnancy and birth of his daughter—the special namesake of her grandmother—really sent me spinning into a horrible depression. Overwrought with anxiety and emotional pain, my depression was full blown.

I made numerous efforts to reach out in different ways to all three of my children and their spouses, only to be ignored completely. I even reached out to Michael's in-laws. In a conversation with his mother-in-law, she declared that she wouldn't assist me with any interventions by reaching out to her daughter. She said that she did not want to be me.

Honestly, to this day, that is one of the saddest and most pathetic things I've heard an adult say: admitting that her daughter and son-in-law had so much control that she was afraid of being cut off like I had been—she didn't want to be me.

After that I made a passionate plea to all three of my adult children asking for their compassion and to please at least communicate with me. I repeated this plea to each one numerous times, and each time it it was ignored. It really made me wonder who these people were that I had raised. They showed no capacity for compassion, forgiveness or sensitivity to my obvious plight. On top of all the other calculated cruelty, this was the moment that became REALLY REALLY bad.

When attending weekly church service, sometimes we would hear readings from *The Book of the All-Virtuous Wisdom of Joshua ben Sira*, commonly called *The Wisdom of Sirach*. I know my children were exposed to it many times. Sirach Chapter 3 involves our duties towards our parents:

Children pay heed to a father's right; do so that you may live. For the Lord sets a father in honor over his children; a mother's authority he confirms over her sons. He who honors his father atones for sins; he stores up riches who reveres his mother.

He who honors his father is gladdened by children, and when he prays he is heard. He who reveres his father will live a long life; he obeys the Lord who brings comfort to his mother. He who fears the Lord honors his father, and serves his parents as rulers.

In word and deed honor your father that this blessing may come upon you; for a father's blessing gives a family strong roots. Glory not in your father's shame, for his shame is no glory to you!

His father's honor is a man's glory; disgrace for her children a mother's shame. My son take care of your father when he is old; grieve him not as long as he lives. Even if his mind fails, be considerate of him; revile him not in the fullness of your strength. For kindness to a father will not be forgotten, it will serve as a sin offering. It will take lasting root. In time of tribulation it will be recalled to your advantage, like warmth against frost it will melt away your sins.

Hydrangea macrophylla

HYDRANGEA

Heartlessness

14

PROFESSIONAL OPINION ...
AND WHAT I BELIEVE

Sometimes children withdraw as they age because of extreme treatment they received in early childhood or adolescence. If this was the case in our family, then the state of our relationship would be easy to understand. If molestation, alcohol abuse, mental or physical brutality had occurred, then extreme reactions later in life might correlate with the major abuse that they lived through. This, however, was not the history with my children.

Their cruel actions and withdrawal from immediate and extended family members are disproportionately extreme in relation to the real or imagined wrongs that they suffered in their youth. Terms like pathological grief, detachment and arrested development are relevant in this situation. I'm convinced it is not any one thing, but a combination of factors (some of which exist only in their own minds) that have been embellished to support a sense of displaced anger and can only be reconciled from within.

In trying to understand the extreme response I've received from three of my adult children I took many things into account. Drawing on experiences and memories of watching them grow, I contemplated some of the complaints or anger they would express and try to interpret what they really meant. This was especially true of expressions they made between their late teens and early thirties, as they each became more expressive with minds of their own. But it's hard to understand exactly what is going on internally both individually or collectively because over the last five years any attempts at an open discussion have been met with unwillingness to communicate.

I also take into consideration their individual personalities. As any parent of multiple children will attest to, children are all unique. Despite being brought up in the same culture, household environment, and being exposed to the same faith, they are different from one another. Varying personalities and outlooks developed even though they share the same DNA and were each afforded the same attention, education and opportunities. Still, I believe they process and regard things differently because they are each at different maturity levels and understanding when a single event happens. Their interpretation is guided by their level of maturity and growth at the particular time. Much like when there has been a car accident and four witnesses relate the details. Authorities confirm that often each accounting of what happened is different from the others regarding the very same accident.

Ever since Swiss American psychiatrist Elisabeth Kübler-Ross's groundbreaking research into the grieving process—the ways in which we grieve the loss of a loved one, or loss in general—the area has mushroomed into a major scientific field of study, and remains one of the most complicated of human experiences. How do we grieve and let go of those we love and what constitutes normal grief?

Dr. Kübler-Ross identified five major stages of grieving: 1) shock, in which the reality of death is difficult to process; 2) denial, in which the reality of the death is refused; 3) anger, in which strong feelings of anger, hostility and even rage can be experienced; 4) bargaining, where an attempt is made to negotiate feelings about the death to alleviate the pain from the loss; and 5) acceptance, in which the reality of the death is realized and integrated.

Generally speaking, the majority of people who experience the death of a loved one will find ways to accept and integrate the loss into their lives within one to seven years. However, for some individuals the grieving process can be delayed, denied, or even become chronic. This is often referred to as pathological grief. Many efforts have been made to study and classify what pathological grief actually is. It has been considered a form of depression, anxiety, post traumatic syndrome or bereavement. Several theoretical formulations have been postulated to explain why some experience this form of grief and others do not.

In his paper "Mourning and Melancholia," Sigmund Freud suggested that during the normal mourning process, the ego unconsciously incorporates characteristics of the object (a loved person) into his or her psyche in an effort to maintain the close relationship with them before eventually submitting to the reality principle and acknowledging the loss. In melancholia, by contrast, investment in the loved person, (based on a memory, idea, or fantasy about that person) which arose in the first place from a narcissistic object choice (a psychological condition characterized by self-preoccupation, lack of empathy, and unconscious deficits in self-esteem) that was originally ambivalent, is withdrawn when the object is lost; but the libido (associated emotional energy), instead of being transferred to other objects, is reinvested in the ego and used to form an unconscious identification with the lost or abandoned object. Object loss becomes ego loss, and the divided ego thereafter maintains a tormented relationship with itself. In other words, those with sound inner working models of healthy caring figures (objects such as parents, friends, relatives) will find ways to integrate the loss. However, if these internal object relations become distorted or impaired, the result could be pathological grief.

While I never wavered and was constantly available to my children, my attempts to move on with another partner and mother figure for my kids—and lack of success in doing so—likely originated this impairment. But as adults now in their thirties, I would expect my children to have gained some perspective and the ability to understand that the issues they may have experienced weren't brought on intentionally and that I did my best while continuing to provide for them and give attention to their needs. I would expect that they would acknowledge the tremendous effort that went into raising four children single-handedly and respond in a mature way rather than with estrangement.

British psychologist John Bowlby suggested viewing grief as an attachment issue. Those with insecure attachments, or a parent who was struggling to maintain healthy attachments at the time of death, will experience the loss as a more severe form of bereavement. This can also work in reverse if a child had a strong attachment to a parent who died early in life. This would certainly apply to all my children as Linda was a fulltime mother and a huge part of their lives. And for my daughter, who was just five at the time, the absence of the main female figure in the family was an especially huge loss. In our case, the remaining parent struggled to maintain healthy attachment behavior after the loss through multiple housekeepers and attempts at family blending. The attachment loss could be experienced as chronic grief or delayed grief later in life. At the adult stage, individuals could experience avoidance of attachment figures, memories, and places that remind them of the attachment figure to avoid dealing with the powerful feelings generated by the loss at an earlier age.

My daughter moved a thousand miles away and refuses any contact with me, her in-laws, aunts, uncles, a sister-in-law that she grew up with as an older sister figure, close college friends, and some siblings of her husband. As for my two younger sons (one who also moved out of state), they do not acknowledge or respond to any aunts, uncles and family friends that have reached out to them—for something even as simple as a seasonal greeting response.

As time goes on, the combination of previously listed factors may lead to delayed grief, and in severe instances can lead to ongoing attachment difficulties, especially with those that remind the bereaved ones of the pain of their loss or the difficulty they had in maintaining a healthy attachment to the remaining caretaker.

Dr. Dan Huber is a clinical psychiatrist with forty years of experience and specializes in child, adolescent, marital and family therapy. He is also the professional with whom I have shared our family's history during countless sessions over the last fifteen years. Dr. Huber illustrated these concepts with possible psychological scenarios and explanations for the complicated ways that grief can express itself, often over the course of a lifetime.

A young parent with four small children is not only shocked, but grief stricken at the loss of what he thought would be his lifelong partner. Doing the best he can, under very stressful circumstances, he decides, with his deceased wife's prior blessings, to pursue other relationships. The intent is positive, that is, to provide a two parent household to raise and support his children emotionally, physically, intellectually and spiritually. Over a series of relationships, tensions begin to arise within the family system. Facing a wall of challenges, the relationships don't work out. Eventually, he finds someone with whom he can enjoy a solid, lasting and loving relationship. The intention is not to replace his initial love, but to provide loving companionship and support for himself and his family.

Prior to this, the young children are experiencing many changes. The worst thing imaginable has happened to them: a parent has died. Being young, the emotions of this event are processed in different ways, mainly with feelings and at times with behaviors, which is the language of children. Being children, they are vulnerable in many ways. First of all, to not want to displease their father (the remaining parent and source of security) by trying initially to form some sense of acceptance to the new mother figure in their lives.

However, a potential conflict exists, in that loyalty to the deceased mother may create confusion and a sense of disloyalty to her by having feelings of attachment and connection to the new mother figure. Again, being vulnerable as young children, these feelings, while experienced internally, may go unexpressed due to the reality of their dependence upon the remaining parent, their father. In some ways, this may interfere with or perhaps even delay normal and age appropriate grieving for their mother. Again, with different replacement mother figures entering the family, starting with the housekeepers, there can be considerable confusion of how to grieve and accept the new realities of their lives without their biological mother.

The father is also in a vulnerable position, in that he naturally wishes the best for his children and tries to maintain some family stability in the process, yet with relationships shifting and changing, he may himself question the effectiveness and advisability of his actions. Further, given temperaments and personality styles, each of the children may experience the introduction of a new mother figure differently. While someone may be fine and adjust; others may struggle for many different reasons. As time goes on and the children mature into adulthood, the feelings generated during the process of re-structuring the family continue. The complication now is that given the circumstances and quality of their burgeoning adult lives, and decreasing dependence on their father, they may begin to experience an opportunity to express repressed or unaddressed feelings of grief generated when their mother died at a young age. Rather than viewing their father as someone who genuinely tried his best under difficult circumstances to maintain family stability and continuity for his family, he may be seen as a villain who, from his children's emotionally time frozen stage and specific point of view, was more concerned with what they perceived he needed rather than what they needed.

Keeping in mind the vulnerability and developmental age at which the initial grief feelings were created, they may not have the window of time and maturity to see the emotional predicament their father was in when their mother died at a young age. Rather than seeing that their father did his best and not use a variety of behavioral tactics to "punish him" for what they may feel as abandoning them after their mother died, they could use this stage of a more empowered adult life to escape having to deal with the sadness of their mother's death and use avoidance of the father as a means to sidestep the process of dealing with a lifetime of repressed grief. Actually, it is beyond avoidance, as it is overt aggression as a means to avoid dealing with their own unresolved grief. Anger is a much easier emotion to express than pain.

Of course, the solution for such a situation would be a candid and adult discussion of the circumstances of the time that their mother died, and use this as an opportunity to rebuild family relationships in a healthy fashion. Unfortunately, this is not always the case, and sadly, estrangement is often employed as a psychological tool to block genuine, painful and repressed grief from emerging. In addition, they are unable to find room to forgive their father for ways they imagined he wronged them and hurt their lives.

I believe that something changed once Jodi passed an imaginary stage within the family. In this case after five years they saw that she was likely committed to me for life. Other relationships barely lasted a year or two as they were up against the family. In contrast, Jodi was not going to withdraw on her own nor was any distance the kids had already shown going to discourage her commitment to the relationship. She was for keeps and she was genuine. I believe in the recesses of their minds this signaled that the family structure was forever changed, something they certainly would have an interest in since their mom passed away. The incident between Lynn and Jodi in no way warranted the firestorm of harsh, angry and vocal lashing out that my youngest two displayed.

I also believe that early on and as time progressed there was always a fear of "If something happened to dad, what would happen to us?" This is a natural concern having already lost their mother. Whether it was a fear they recognized or not I don't fully know because they won't express what it really is that angers them. But in a strange way of self-fulfilled prophecy and fear they have rejected me and my spouse at a time in their lives when they have secured their own partners and they believe they would never have to depend on me for any kind of love and security again. I believe this dynamic may also play a part in their choice to withdraw. These are all plausible reasons with science that supports them.

I also believe that the life they lived—which by most standards would be considered privileged—also fed into a sense of entitlement, just as it seems to have for many of their generation. They certainly were blessed with opportunities including education and financial assistance as they each entered adult life debt free, college degree paid for, with a new car and a significant down payment for their first house, allowing them to build immediate equity. I believe even before they were at that age I had given attention and support over and above the average setting. I know I did this in a subconscious way to make up for their tragic loss while young. But I believe I over-provided and over-excused in cases that might have warranted a bit more discipline. They were especially unwilling when it came to any attempts to blend families and at the end were always judgmental and un-accepting of any offspring that came with the person I tried to establish a life with. That behavior most recently extended to Jodi's daughters. In looking back, they always acted superior to the children brought into the blended family, with arrogant words and actions. Their sense of proprietary position was obvious throughout the years. In looking back, they were not open or willing to share what they felt was theirs and their father's, which included their father's attention. One can only imagine how much more difficult this made an already difficult situation.

I also believe that despite all my efforts and attention amidst the challenges I faced as a single parent of four, that they felt a need for more love. I wish I would have hugged them more and was able to emit the love that only a mother can provide, but I did the best I could in tending to their needs while most of the time being sleep deprived and running on empty. I believe their need for verbal affirmation and physical expressions of love over and above the encouragement I gave them regularly was a void in them. I can't help but believe that when I see their lack of empathy and compassion towards me and the same lack of feeling for their older brother, his wife and other close relatives.

As we are often encouraged by people of wisdom, "Hug your child when you arrive home today." My life's experience and wisdom encourages the same. I suspect that most parents ultimately feel the same when all said and done: that they could have done more. It is that insatiable feeling a parent is somehow left with no matter what their contribution was.

I also believe that the attempts to make our family whole again were doomed from the beginning. No matter who I would have introduced at the time, they would have ultimately been met with rejection. I've acknowledged that I should have been more patient and taken more time in my selection process, which could have possibly resulted in better choices. But with all that was going on, I just wanted things fixed and to be whole as a family again. Their ultimate rejection of my choices over the years wasn't just of my partner but of the children they brought with them. The thing that gives me some solace is that even as adults with none of the conflicts that can develop while living under the same roof, my three younger children still rejected Jodi and her daughters. This occurred at a time when their thinking should have been more mature, more accepting and less emotional and when there weren't any true conflicts to point to. Still, they cruelly rejected Jodi and her daughters too. However, Jodi is as good as they come—I couldn't have done better. This leads me to believe it was the complete dynamic including all involved that made it impossible. No doubt my choices were challenged because there were four of them—a challenging package for anyone. But having said that, in the spirit of meeting them part way I have apologized to my children many times over the years for my part in moving too quickly in trying to complete the family. They do not accept this apology, but instead remain angry with closed hearts. I've told them often that "forgiveness is the best gift you can give yourself" but with very little empathy they are unable to receive that message.

All this leads me to believe that they have a displaced anger and that they are emotionally stunted. Their cruel actions are simply out of line and unreasonable in connection with the events of the past. Their deeds have been more hurtful than I can ever express. Having my grandchildren withheld makes me feel like the victim of a crime. In fact, in the United States, grandparents have a legal right to visit with their grandchildren. Even though I try to give them the benefit of doubt, as I did most of the time I was raising them, there is no denying what they are doing is wrong. When I think of the fact that one grandchild I have only been allowed to see on his day of birth and another one I've seen on only two occasions within the first 4 months(when I look at that grandchild's picture from three years ago whom I haven't been allowed to see since)I know I've missed that precious infant and toddler time and it greatly saddens me, and that there are two other grandchildren that I have never met at all, well it breaks my heart. It breaks my heart for myself, for the loss the grandchild has in not knowing what they are missing, and for their parents as they are robbed of seeing their children's joy that only comes with a grandchild-grandparent relationship. It's a relationship that I have known for the last thirteen years enjoying the growth of my oldest son's four children. That joy inevitably reminds me of what is missing with the other five grandchildren. It is a living nightmare when I realize what my children and their spouses have intentionally done with their estrangement. Using their children as a weapon is beyond belief and reason … and desperately sad for all of us.

What I know is the natural and loving relationship that exists with the four grandchildren that we are close to. It is the one where their faces beam with our arrival. I'm certain it is the reflection of the beaming faces of Grandma and Grandpa. I see their excitement as they wait for us to open our luggage to find out what treat we brought along for them this time: is it a puzzle, a bag of Twizzlers, slippers, a new swimming suit or some kind of learning device with letters or numbers? I know the feeling of connectedness as we do the "secret handshake" that only we share. The feeling of picking them up from school on Friday and getting a McFlurry to celebrate a tradition Grandpa introduced to them: T.G.I.F. I know the joy of watching a favorite movie with them like The Princess Bride and now forever when they ask for something with a "please," my response is "As you wish." In the movie the term "as you wish" really meant "I love you." So we say this to our grandchildren now and it's our little fun. Or the anticipation as they visit our Florida vacation home and we measure their height against the board to see how much they have grown since the last visit. Or looking forward to the next Camp Team George event (CTG) with fishing, tubing, swimming, campfires, s'mores, ghost stories, basketball, motorized cars, ice cream sundaes and a different color t-shirt memorializing that particular year of CTG. And more smiles and food for the soul than I could ever remember each time we see their faces.

This is all the love and fun that is being forfeited by the parents of the other five grandchildren. Someday I believe that forfeiture will result in regret, or even jealousy, if it hasn't already, as they witness other grandparent relationships of their friends or if they ever learn of what their own experiences could have been. But, of course, they will blame that void on me because that is all they can do. I believe they may never have the courage to take responsibility for the estrangement they have dictated. Someday, though, their children will see pictures or hear first hand from their cousins about what it was like to be with Grandma and Grandpa. How will they feel when they find out what they missed? Who will they blame?

We may never get to explore the joy and pleasure of getting to know these five precious grandchildren, but through the time we've spent with the four children of my oldest son, we can only imagine how wonderful it would be. Of course, these five little people will not know what they are missing. And their parents, my children, will never get to witness the incredible joy of their children and the joy of their parents because they have blocked it. They blocked it from conception, precluding sharing the pregnancy journey by either shutting me out or simply not making us aware of the pregnancy. They precluded any connection by not sharing the day of the blessed birth. This is formative time beginning with the pregnancy and reinforced during infancy and as toddlers can never be reconstructed. This is when the bond of unconditional love and trust of grandparents originates. I believe this is when the emotional attachment is embedded. If you show up years later in their life you are simply introduced as a person with a name of Grandpa. It might as well be Tom or Joe. All association with the emotion that could have been established is forfeited. This is the part that is really really bad knowing it has already passed by and there is nothing to be done to make it good. And it is made especially challenging because four of the five being held hostage from us are out of state, reducing easy access opportunities.

On a positive note, in the summer of 2013, my wife's daughter, Brooke, and her husband, brought a beautiful little girl into the world. It was a pregnancy we delighted in following all the way right up until the point where Jodi was invited into the delivery room and joined her daughter and son-in-law for a memory she will never forget: witnessing the miracle of life. This process is what a parent and grandparent lives for, but for me it was also a painful reminder of what some of my children selfishly withheld by using these blessed happenings as weapons to punish me.

Putting all of this into perspective I also believe that if we all threw our problems in life into a pile and saw everyone else's, we'd grab ours back. While I don't have to embrace these problems, I do have to accept them and view them as challenges because they are just that, and they are my life. No one is in charge of my happiness except me. I can't compare my life to others because I have no idea what their journey is all about. And as we've heard many times, unless you've walked in someone's shoes, you have no idea what their experience has been. In the words of the philosopher Friedrich Nietzsche, and echoed in a popular song by Kelly Clarkson: "What doesn't kill you makes you stronger." Stronger is what we need to be. I'm reminded of something Linda would say during her last months, "It's just the hand we are dealt."

Even as I record these words and you read them, and as I continually try to convince myself of their truth, it doesn't make it easier. In fact, it is just the opposite. This is, without a doubt, the hardest time of my life, and what is really really bad.

God never promises to remove our struggles. He does, however, promise to change the way we look at them, and in that process we will see everything differently.

Galanthus Nivalis

SNOWDROP

Hope

15

SURVIVING THE DARKNESS:
AN ONGOING PROCESS

Everything that slows us down and forces patience, everything that sets us back into the slow circles of nature, is a help. Gardening is an instrument of grace. —— May Sarton

The more attention, care, love, time and overall investment you've put into your children—especially with so much of the time functioning as a mother and father—the further you have to fall into the dark pit of estrangement. Depressed feelings start early when the rejection begins. Being made to stand outside someone's home when you come to visit; the irony being that ownership of that home would not have been possible without the down payment I gifted them. The depression from rejection continues to build when they don't return phone calls, block phone calls, and return letters and gifts for the grandkids. Then they move far away and won't give you a forwarding address. The hurt and depression elevates to another level as they refuse to even send updated pictures of the grandkids and then shield pregnancies of future grandkids as well as the births, as happened on two different occasions in 2012. At this point hurt and depression is so deep I can barely see the sky above the pit.

The pain and anxiety this all creates is never ending. These are your children that you have raised and have always had the responsibility of caring for and now they are intentionally hurting you. The relationship is primal and their hurtful intentional actions make little sense. There is no arguing that nothing is more important than family. With the imposed estrangement blocking all opportunities to communicate, it leaves me helpless and hopeless. At this point I need to seek help from to a higher place.

One's faith needs to be the cornerstone; pray and pray some more. A wise friend once said that when you pray, the answers to your prayers are yes, no and not yet time. Being a man of faith, I rely on that faith—the very faith I exposed all my children to, and the same faith that was even more important to their mother. I regularly light my novena candles, pray to St. Jude, patron of the impossible, and possess an invaluable class A relic (an actual bone fragment of St. Jude) that I received from a very dear priest friend who had it willed to him when one of his parishioners died. Think of it: St. Jude walked with Jesus!

I also sought professional assistance from a family therapist. I confided in my closest friends and family, although they would find out anyway over time in asking about the well being of the kids—I wasn't going to lie or make things up; they deserve better. I found confiding in them to be somewhat helpful in sharing my circumstances with people that genuinely care the most. I've also tried to selectively distract myself with life. This hasn't been easy though, because of the constant reminders of what my children have done. Most of all I feel very fortunate to have an incredibly loving partner in my spouse: my biggest blessing and earthly assistance. If you have this kind of special person in your life you should cry with them. It's more healing than crying alone. Another way I've tried to move out of the funk was to write about it in this book, and that has been very cathartic. The pain and hurt never disappears, but I try to find ways to manage it rather than letting it manage and define who I am.

Most importantly, I believe if you can take people's anger, you can heal people. I have chosen this path. Our natural tendency is to respond to anger with anger of our own. Actually, though, the people who vent their anger on you are seldom actually angry at you. They are expressing their anger to you, so it feels like you are their target. The natural response to being attacked is retaliation. After all, we are programmed for self preservation. But if you can field their anger without becoming defensive—definitely easier said than done—you will nearly always discover that you are not the true object of their hostility. If you can hear their anger quietly and sympathetically, you may set them on the road to healing. If you can take peoples anger, you have a shot at healing them.

I have tried most everything else, and as a benefit of the ingrained unconditional love of a parent I have been able to adopt this thinking, although its success is yet to be seen. That's not to say it is easy by any means or diffuses the hurt I feel, but this is where my faith and the power of prayer comes in. I need to try to heal myself and exert a passive approach, even if I can't deliver an immediate cure for the children I love.

In quoting Jesus, Matthew 5:44 reads, "But I say to you, love your enemies and those that do you wrong, and pray for those who persecute and hurt you."

Really? Pray for those who hurt me? How about I just pray for my friends? But the healing begins precisely in the discomfort of trying to implement that verse. Our obedience is a sign to God that we are finally ready to grow. We agree that we are willing to leave our own (unsuccessful) methods behind and relinquish all our past hurts and resentments into God's capable hands. Make peace with your past so it won't damage your present. When we pray for those who hurt us, we experience what I view as a boomerang blessing: it touches our target then returns to us, hitting the exact place where we are most broken. It finally becomes easier to breathe. Our wounds begin to heal cleanly. We are able to see those who hurt us with more compassion. Our hard hearts are softened. We are changed.

In praying, I not only pray for myself and my family, but more importantly I pray for others. I believe in praying we receive waves of grace that help sustain us. It helps mitigate the waves of grief we experience. I also believe when you pray it releases healing. Prayer is God touching our soul—what better therapy could there be? And "praying it forward" it is much like paying it forward. When you pray for someone else and their needs it is a natural distraction and takes the focus off your own hardship, if even only for a little while. It's just good practice and a random act of kindness to "pray it forward. "

Patience and faith are very important. How many times have we heard this suggested? But it is true. Healing doesn't come until there is communication, understanding and a willingness to open one's heart. This could happen in months or years; it is impossible to know without two lines of communication. And during this time I'll have to entertain the possibility that this situation might never be reconciled, as hard as it is to accept. It might never happen in your lifetime. If I can find a way to get to this point in acceptance, I have just taken back control of my life, because now the fear of this happening no longer holds me hostage. For an optimist like me, this is very difficult to accept because it also means giving up hope in a sense. But when I've really come to realize that I have little or no control I am closer to peace. And yes giving up hope can put me on a slippery slope to being distraught, which can be very dark. That is when and why I pray. Not for myself but for the well being of my family. After all, that is ultimately what I care about and it is what was my mission was from day one in bringing them into the world. It is a selfless and unconditional love that is my strength and, of course, my weakness when the anxiety overwhelms me.

Many people believe they have plenty of time left on the game clock, and for sure at the latest they can gather the courage to do the right thing—certainly by the time there is a death bed. Except, as we know all too well, life is fragile and fleeting, and no one is guaranteed a death bed. Like the flame of a candle, the flicker of life can be blown out in an instant.

It's okay to have hope, but only a realistic hope. Otherwise, we can be setting ourselves up for disappointment and failure.

Also, lowered expectations can reduce the chances of disappointment. Lowered expectations put you on a clearer path to peace. Pray. Keep the faith and when the time is right, all can come back to the center. And most always: love. As the Apostle Paul wrote," There is faith, hope and love, but the greatest of these is love." You can't go wrong with this combination. It might take a little time to get used to this approach. Kind of like your body adjusting to an antidepressant. But this organic way of getting to peace is the high road to getting what you really need and want. It certainly isn't the easy path; it is a never-ending challenge. And unfortunately, there's no short cut or secret pill. But when it is hard, know that it is normal, and hopefully each difficult episode will get you closer to the end of the tunnel where there is light to be seen, and where hope and anticipation meet and welcome you to just a little more peace than you had yesterday. Unlike a crash diet, where you quickly put the weight back on, this slow and steady approach requires patience and commitment, and like most successful ventures, is centered on behavioral modification including the way you think about and approach your grief.

But critical to healing is forgiving and letting go. It begins with forgiving. In Luke 6:37 it reads, "Forgive and you will be forgiven." For me, there are two hard parts about forgiving. One is that it can feel like I'm approving of what my children have done to me. I believe this is why some people say "I'll forgive but I won't forget." But I'm not sure that is true forgiveness. The other hard part is that being offended gives one a sense of importance that the humility of forgiveness removes. To truly forgive someone means that I let go of being better than the person and their actions that offended or hurt me. It means letting go of being righteous in favor of being loving. You can focus on being right or on being kind. It's nearly impossible to do both at the same time all the time. It reminds me of when a wife kiddingly asks her husband, "Do you want to be right or happy?" It takes deep humility to forgive. In forgiveness we practice kindness, and we hope that such kindness will be returned to us.

It can start with a random act of kindness that can never be known or acknowledged by others. Perhaps a prayer in behalf of someone you know or don't know: that they have a better day and find their path to peace. Time heals almost everything—almost. Allow time and that it is acceptable to believe in miracles—except when playing the lottery; save your miracles for the things that really matter.

All that truly matters in the end is that you loved. And there are many ways to love. For the last few years I loved by chasing and doing what men do: trying to fix things. My belief was that if I tried to help my adult children see and understand what I have discovered through much professional assistance, that they would have an epiphany at some point. But after banging my head against the wall and taking the high road, trying to deflect but more often wearing their barbs of meanness and disrespect, I realize that my passive action and willingness to be beaten up and rejected was only empowering them. They each became more convinced that they had all the answers, when in reality they had very few of the answers.

In continuing to love them—as I will until long after I leave this earth—I will love them at a distance. It's true that distance may feed into their belief that their father abandoned them, just as they always imagined that I did at some level in their mind. And true, with that distance, I won't be able to offer that convenient return from them when they are ready. I will just have to rely upon them having the needed courage to communicate when they have finally reached that point. That is blind faith, but it's what I have concluded after enduring the emotional storm down to this day. I still believe with my whole being that all that really matters is that you love while mustering the confidence to believe that better days will come.

For me, some days are still darker than others, and some are still gray. But I learned that you need to truly live life with a grateful heart for all the blessings we are privileged with, including but not limited to our health, our eyesight, the beautiful sights of God's creation, our family and friends that love and treasure us, our functioning brain, our ability to reason, our interest in kindness and compassion and all the gifts that make up our being, and of course, the gift of life itself. If we can remind ourselves of this gratitude during those moments we humanly take for granted, then we have a chance to wait out the storms in our lives with patience. We need to look at life from thirty thousand feet and have appreciation of life from a wide angle lens, rather than allowing something that we can't control and its deep rooted sadness to dominate our view.

I will quietly wait for the return of the garden I knew when the children were younger and we moved as a team to nurture growth from this plot that has now become overgrown with vines and weeds which have strangled and sucked the life out of all that was good and growing. And after I've let the garden soil lay fallow with my patience, faith, and hope, I will anticipate the day when what was really really bad withers from memory and the broad leaves and vibrant colors of happiness, peace and love return and come into full and joyous bloom.

A garden is a grand teacher. It teaches patience and careful watchfulness; it teaches industry and thrift; above all it teaches entire trust. — *Unknown*

EPILOGUE

When we are young and we hear of *Faith*, *Hope* and *Love*, they may seem to be just lofty words strewn together. But as our lives unfold, each word takes on a new and separate meaning—and a life of its own. In the garden that is life we come to more fully understand this trio: the importance of *Hope*, the meaning of *Faith*, and above all, the power of *Love*. If all we learn and do is *Love*, we win.

In my garden of interconnections I am blessed with wonderful siblings, many good friends and a life partner that truly is my best half. As we all continue to grow alongside each other, I keep striving to live a faith filled life full of love and appreciation.

ABOUT THE AUTHOR

Thomas George was born and raised in the upper Midwestern United States as part of a family of ten. He married his high school sweetheart at age twenty and they welcomed their first child just two years later. After college he briefly taught high school students and worked for a major soft drink company before landing in the radio business by way of an independent marketing and sales venture. After thirty-three years in the radio business—twenty-eight as the President and General Manager of a successful local cluster of five stations—he chose the elective life that retirement offers with the intention of spending the third act of his life enjoying the company of his adult children and grandchildren while also spending time playing tennis, traveling and seeking outreach opportunities. In retirement he has taken on an occasional radio consulting challenge with his primary domicile still only a half hour from where he grew up.

Thomas George can be contacted via email at the following address:

HeathfieldPublishing@gmail.com

22869971R00114

Made in the USA
San Bernardino, CA
26 July 2015